Mastering Basic Skills™

Fourth Grade

Helping Children Succeed!

ISBN 1-60022-081-9

Table of Contents

Table of Contents

Contents by Skill

Contents by Skill

Phonics

Pull-out Mini-Books

Reading Comprehension

Introduction

Welcome to *Mastering Basic Skills*. Fourth grade often marks the end of elementary school. At this age, children are maturing, able to set standards for themselves, and developing personal interests and talents. Fourth graders are learning to use their academic skills as life skills. They are reading for knowledge and enjoyment, using real-world math skills and discovering an increased ability to communicate through the written word.

For some children, fourth grade also marks the emergence of the preteen. This can mean that you might begin to see moodiness and some rebellious behaviors. Children at this age are trying to grow up and become more independent. We want children to think independently and to act critically and responsibly. To accomplish this, children need to put some distance between themselves and their parents. Do not let this distancing behavior alarm you. Instead, try to understand it and keep the lines of communication open. Encourage sharing. Ask questions. Be ready to listen.

Emerging preteens also need to be surrounded by a positive environment. Instead of constantly reminding her to complete tasks or reprimanding her when you think she is wrong, try finding moments throughout the day when you say only positive comments to your child. Children need your support and encouragement now, even more than when she was little. Provide an atmosphere that will promote open and honest communication.

Friends are becoming increasingly more important. Children are developing social skills and are now able to engage in group decision-making. You will also find that many fourth graders have developed a great sense of truthfulness—they can be incredibly honest. This is a trait that we want to last forever!

Fourth grade children are getting ready to take that leap into more abstract thinking. For this reason, it is vital that children have developed a solid foundation of basic skills. The skill review provided in this book helps strengthen that foundation for further school success—and it is fun!

Everyday Ways to Enrich Learning Experiences

Language Arts

The single most important skill that a child needs for success in school, and later in life, is to be "literate." In other words, children must learn how to read. You can do many things to encourage literacy.

- Encourage your child to read every day, whether it be books, magazines, short stories, or poetry.
- Read the same books your child is reading so you can share the stories together. Talk about what is going to happen next, have your child make up a new ending for the story, and discuss the characters, plot, and setting.
- Go to the library and let your child choose new books.
- Write a story together. Have your child illustrate the story.
- Have your child make a comic book.
- Fill your child's environment with literacy materials like books, magazines, newspapers, catalogs, paper, pencils, crayons, paints, and music CDs.
- Encourage your child to write thank-you notes or letters.
- Together make a scrapbook of fourth-grade memories.
- Supervise your child's use of the Internet. Search for stories, games, and learning activities that your child can enjoy online. (See Web sites, page 9.)
- Take your child to a play or some type of theatrical production.
- Encourage your child to read and write poetry.
- Ask your child to look through the newspaper for information: weather, sports, local events, national news, comics, and movie listings.
- Have your child make her own address and phone directory.

Math and Science

So many toys and puzzles provide children with early math and science learning experiences. Remember to point out all the ways we use numbers and science in our daily lives. Here are some suggested materials and activities:

- Get your child a watch and encourage telling time and being on time.
- Provide blocks, puzzles, and other building materials.
- Encourage play with magnets, scales, and science books and kits.
- Have your child practice using numbers "in his head" (mental math).
- Help your child learn basic math facts. Play math games. (See Web sites, page 9.)
- Play card games. This can help children learn to add quickly.
- Play games with your child. Trivia, word, math, and problem-solving games can make for a fun family evening.
- Visit science, art, and history museums.
- Discuss how we use numbers in the real world.
- Encourage your child to begin a hobby. Encourage individual interests.
- Encourage an interest in music.

Fun Web Sites for Fourth Graders

http://www.bookadventure.org/ki/index.asp
> The "Book Finder" helps kids find books at a particular reading level and on specific topics chosen by the child. Some site features require free registration.

http://www.childrensmuseum.org/games/grades_3-5.html
> At this interactive site, kids can learn about living in space, create a multimedia project, solve science mysteries, and play online games. The Children's Museum of Indianapolis maintains this Web site.

http://www.coolmath4kids.com
> This colorful site offers interactive math games, puzzles, math tricks, and calculators. Topics include whole number operations, tessellations, fractions, geometry, logic problems, algebra, and probability. At this fun site, kids can practice math skills and learn about fascinating math concepts.

http://www.factmonster.com
> Lots and lots of facts are offered at this Web site. Visitors can learn about countries and people, the United States, math concepts, sports, and science topics such as stars and planets, weather, animals, and the human body. Interactive educational games as well as arcade games and a homework center are included.

http://funbrain.com/kidscenter.html
> Site features a variety of interactive games with multiple skill levels that cover math, language arts, and science concepts. Visitors can practice math facts, rounding numbers and identifying place value, reading comprehension and spelling skills, and much more.

http://www.kidshealth.org/kid/
> At this site, kids can read about dealing with feelings in different situations, find out about caring for their bodies to stay healthy, and take an interactive tour of the systems of the body. Other health topics are included. A search can be done for specific questions.

http://www.kidskonnect.com
> This safe Internet gateway for kids offers an extensive list of links to informative Web sites. Categories include animals, countries, games and puzzles, geography, health, holidays and seasons, language arts, math, museums, music, people, sports, states, transportation, and others.

http://www.missmaggie.org
> Animated stories and interactive games introduce kids to real-life environmental problems at this Web site. As kids complete each Earth Adventure mission, they apply math, science, language arts and problem-solving skills.

http://www.nasa.gov/audience/forstudents/k-4/home/index.html
> This site is sponsored by NASA and offers puzzles, games, and science stories. Kids can learn about the space shuttle, rockets and airplanes, the Space Station, stars, and much more. Fun project ideas and activities are included.

http://www.nationalgeographic.com/kids/
> Site includes fun facts, coloring pages, games, homework help, and maps. Also provides a link to the online edition of National Geographic for Kids.

http://www.ology.amnh.org/index.html
> This interactive site will introduce kids to dinosaurs and fossils, the planets and the Milky Way, and other science topics. Kids are encouraged to collect "Ology" cards that feature fun facts, learn about the work of a paleontologist and an astronomer, read stories, solve puzzles, and play games. The site is maintained by the American Museum of Natural History in New York City.

http://www.thunk.com
> At this fun Web site, kids can change their words into secret messages for friends to unscramble. Links to FBI for Kids, CIA for Kids, and science Web sites are provided.

http://www.urbanext.uiuc.edu/kids/index.html
> Site features interactive activities about planning and caring for a garden, how foods grow, earthworms, and getting along with people. Kids can play games, read short stories, and learn interesting facts to understand the mysteries of plant life and the importance of earthworms.

http://www.wordcentral.com
> Learning new words can be fun. At this site, kids find out about new words by reading the "Daily Buzzword," discover how words get into the dictionary, and look up words to find out their meanings. This site is maintained by Merriam-Webster.

Cursive Letter Practice

Trace and write the cursive letters.

Aa   Bb   Cc

Dd   Ee   Ff

Gg   Hh   Ii

Jj   Kk   Ll

Mm   Nn

Oo   Pp   Qq

Rr   Ss   Tt

Uu   Vv   Ww

Xx   Yy   Zz

Cursive Writing Evaluation

Copy the poem in your best cursive handwriting.

There was a rabbit

With a bad habit

Of jumping on places

Like crocodiles' faces!

Matching Vowel Sounds

Draw a line to connect each word in the first column with a word in the second column that has the **same vowel sound**.

ax	big
cool	cat
cup	led
egg	pay
lake	school
like	smile
lit	toll
load	up

Identifying Place Value

Write the **place value** of the highlighted digit on the line.
The first one has been done for you.

A. 8,567,123   ten thousands _____

B. 7,400,205   _____

C. 5,952,631   _____

D. 2,540,513   _____

E. 4,521,368   _____

F. 2,261,968   _____

G. 4,231,948   _____

Standard Form Notation

Write each number in **standard form.**

A. 500 + 90 + 6 _____

B. 2,000 + 400 + 60 + 7 _____

C. 40,000 + 3,000 + 800 + 20 + 1 _____

D. 200,000 + 50,000 + 7,000 + 10 + 4 _____

E. Write your own. _____

Dictionary Pronunciation

Listen to the vowel sounds in each word below. Draw a line
to connect each word with its **dictionary pronunciation.**

dream	(āt)
knot	(pĭk´ əl)
shirt	(rīt)
crew	(shûrt)
officer	(kŏm´ ət)
tense	(drēm)
write	(kroo͞)
mermaid	(mûr´ mād)
pickle	(nŏt)
eight	(ŏ´ f ə sûr)
comet	(tĕns)

Beginning Consonant Blends

Look at the **consonant blends** in the box below. Write a blend on each line to form a word that matches one of the pictures. Draw a line from the word to its picture.

cl	dr	sc	sk	sn	st

1. _____ake

2. _____oud

3. _____ess

4. _____ared

5. _____unk

6. _____ore

7. _____amp

8. _____um

9. _____irt

10. _____ock

Rounding Numbers

Round each number to the nearest **ten**.

A. 6,388 _____

B. 567,912 _____

C. 1,587,561 _____

D. 89,258 _____

Round each number to the nearest **hundred**.

E. 8,258 _____

F. 553 _____

G. 22,025 _____

H. 2,364 _____

Round each number to the nearest **thousand**.

I. 10,589 _____

J. 23,278 _____

K. 654,342 _____

L. 32,751 _____

Understanding Place Value

Write the **place value** of the highlighted digit on the line.
The first one has been done for you.

A.   3,921   _____hundreds_____   B.   1,572   _____

C.   2,463   _____   D.   5,761   _____

E.   4,984   _____   F.   1,756   _____

G.   6,357   _____   H.   6,852   _____

Complete the Sentence

Use the words from the word list to complete the sentences below.

Word List

insists	blend	borrow	dangerous
entire	proud	amazing	fond

1. The acrobats at the circus do _____ tricks.

2. Jan is _____ of her new classmate, Diana.

3. When you _____ blue and yellow, you get green.

4. Mom always _____ that I wear my seat belt.

5. Playing in the street can be _____ .

6. I was _____ when I won first prize.

7. May I _____ your eraser?

8. Sarah drank the _____ carton of milk.

Ending Consonant Blends

Choose a **consonant blend** from the word list to complete a different word on each line.

1. ba_____

2. la_____

3. la_____

4. si_____

5. tru_____

6. ca_____

7. da_____

8. da_____

9. de_____

Word List

ft	sp
mp	nd
nk	nt
	st

10. ba_____

11. la_____

12. si_____

13. tru_____

14. tru_____

15. ca_____

16. da_____

17. de_____

18. cri_____

Understanding Place Value

Write the **place value** of the highlighted digit in the box.

A. 47,629

B. 35,116

C. 59,024

D. 23,199

E. 98,965

F. 78, 620

G. 83,456

H. 19,201

A Friendly Letter

Write a letter to your favorite actor or actress. Include all five parts of a friendly letter. Remember to put a comma after the greeting and closing.

_____

_____

_____

_____

_____

_____

_____

_____

_____

Addressing an Envelope

Address the envelope below using the information given.

The sender is:
Mr. Fred Barrow
216 Dawson Drive
Ogden, UT 66065

The receiver is:
Ms. Carla George
22 W. 42nd Street
Tampa, FL 21563

_____

_____

_____

_____

_____

_____

Identifying Types of Stories

Read each title below. Write **F** on the line if you believe the story is **fiction**,
NF if you think it is **nonfiction**, or **B** if you think it is a **biography**.

_____ 1. Kelly's Rainbow Zebra

_____ 2. Life in Jamestown

_____ 3. How Cars Are Made

Fiction:	a story that is made-up or is not factual
Nonfiction:	a true or factual story
Biography:	a story about a real person's life

_____ 4. We Rode on a Unicorn

_____ 5. Plants of North America

_____ 6. The Life of Albert Einstein

_____ 7. My Trip to Mars

_____ 8. Lincoln, the Sixteenth President

_____ 9. Georgie, the Singing Monkey

_____ 10. All about Susan B. Anthony

_____ 11. The Battles of the Civil War

_____ 12. The 10,000-Year-Old Woman

Silent Letters

Draw a circle around the **silent letter** or **letters** in each word.

1. know	2. comb	3. kneel	4. light
5. ghastly	6. write	7. gnaw	8. wrap
9. gnat	10. knife	11. gnome	12. knock
13. knot	14. thumb	15. climb	16. tomb
17. wrench	18. knit	19. dough	20. knight
21. knee	22. gnu	23. wrist	24. gnarl

Two-Digit Addition

Circle the **even** answers. Draw a square around the **odd** answers.

A. 86 + 45	B. 62 + 95	C. 81 + 55	D. 37 + 87	E. 64 + 56
F. 50 + 58	G. 65 + 70	H. 98 + 14	I. 88 + 58	J. 94 + 21
K. 54 + 87	L. 54 + 64	M. 73 + 15	N. 82 + 41	O. 33 + 45

Abbreviations

Write the correct abbreviation for each on the line beside it.
Use the abbreviations word list.

Apartment _____   Railroad _____   centimeter _____

Avenue _____   Road _____   Department _____

Boulevard _____   dozen _____   teaspoon _____

Building _____   Junior _____   hour _____

Word List

Bldg.	cm	tsp.	Apt.	Jr.	Ave.
Blvd.	Dept.	hr.	RR	dz.	Rd.

Classifying

Read the words in each box. Circle the word that **does not belong** with the others.

seven forty fork sixteen	July December Monday February
flour sugar milk kitchen	movie letter magazine book
owl kangaroo cantaloupe wolf	black house orange yellow

Following Directions

Follow the directions to draw a picture in the box.

1. Draw a tree with four branches and orange and red leaves in the bottom left corner.
2. Draw a yellow half moon in the upper right corner.
3. Draw a brown fence across the bottom.
4. Draw four gray cats on the fence.
5. Draw six dark clouds in the sky.
6. Draw one owl on a branch of the tree.
7. Draw five black birds flying in the sky.
8. Add any other details you wish.

Break the Code

Find the sums. Write the letter next to each problem on the correct lines below to read the coded message.

(I)
$$96 + 58$$

(V)
$$56 + 86$$

(D)
$$79 + 38$$

(E)
$$86 + 27$$

(K)
$$38 + 87$$

(D)
$$64 + 83$$

(U)
$$89 + 47$$

(G)
$$58 + 62$$

(A)
$$73 + 49$$

(Y)
$$86 + 76$$

(W)
$$69 + 52$$

(R)
$$77 + 54$$

142 113 131 162   120 147 147 117   121 147 131 125

Categories of Words

Circle the three words that belong together in a category.

1.
golf   lawyer

artist   doctor

2.
train   car

airplane   glove

3.
lungs   brain

heart   food

4.
Canada   Texas

Virginia   Florida

5.
necklace   ring

balloon   bracelet

6.
happy   grumpy

embarrassed   laughter

Alphabetical Order

Write numbers in front of the words in each group to put them in **alphabetical order**.

A.

king

keen

kernel

knee

keep

kind

kangaroo

B.

toast

toffee

told

tomorrow

total

together

tough

C.

egg

elephant

ensemble

elf

electric

ending

especially

Using Math Symbols <, >, or =

Solve each problem. Print the answer next to the correct letter at the bottom.
Place the correct symbol (<, >, or =) in the circle.

A. 22 + 35 = _____   B. 60 + 39 = _____   C. 50 + 31 = _____

D. 63 + 20 = _____   E. 10 + 3 = _____   F. 50 + 25 = _____

G. 77 + 7 = _____   H. 60 + 21 = _____   I. 12 + 30 = _____

_____ ◯ _____
(A)   (G)

_____ ◯ _____
(B)   (I)

_____ ◯ _____
(D)   (G)

_____ ◯ _____
(C)   (H)

_____ ◯ _____
(F)   (E)

_____ ◯ _____
(A)   (G)

Cloze

Read the story below. Many words are missing.
Fill in the blanks with words from the word list.

Randy loved to paint. He liked to paint with his fingers _____
he was little. He would paint on _____. He would paint on
tables. Once he _____ painted on the living room wall!
Randy's _____ were not happy with his painting. They _____
_____ him to play ball or ride his _____,
but Randy only wanted to paint. When _____ was older, he
helped the neighbors paint _____ house. He painted
a huge but beautiful _____ on the front of their house. The
_____ did not want a huge, beautiful flower
_____ on the front of their house. Randy _____
that job! Today Randy is very happy. _____ is a famous
painter. Now his parents _____ his painting. And the
neighbors wish they still had the flower on the front of their house.

Word List

begged
bicycle
even
flower
He
lost
love
neighbors
painted
paper
parents
Randy
their
when

Three-Digit Addition

Add to solve each problem.

A.   486
    + 514

B.   237
    + 185

C.   902
    + 404

D.   375
    + 612

E.   842
    + 254

F.   951
    + 726

G.   33
      76
    + 54

H.   45
      48
    + 85

Addition with Decimals

Add to solve each problem.

A.   3.5
   + 8.2

B.   7.9
   + 3.1

C.   9.0
   + 4.8

D.   49.5
   + 52.4

E.   7.03
   + 7.85

F.   3.25
   + 4.94

G.   8.03
   + 5.13

H.   49.6
   + 31.2

Syllables

Read the animal names below. Count the number
of **syllables** in each name. Print the number of syllables in the box.

rabbit ☐   snake ☐   elephant ☐

monkey ☐   lion ☐   giraffe ☐

flamingo ☐   manatee ☐   dinosaur ☐

koala ☐   wolverine ☐   dolphin ☐

whale ☐   aardvark ☐   emu ☐

Writing Paragraphs

Read the title and main idea of the paragraph. Write your own details.

Title of paragraph: My Best Friend

Main Idea: My best friend is someone special.

Details:

1. _____

2. _____

3. _____

4. _____

Retell the Main Idea: I am glad I have such a great friend.

Use the information above to write a paragraph. Include the main idea and details, then retell the main idea. Indent the first sentence. Use capital letters and periods. Remember to title the paragraph.

_____

_____

_____

_____

_____

_____

_____

_____

Days of the Week Abbreviations

Write the **abbreviation** for each day of the week.
Then find each word in the word search below.

1. Sunday _____

2. Friday _____

3. Thursday _____

4. Saturday _____

5. Monday _____

6. Wednesday _____

7. Tuesday _____

```
M  O  N  D  A  Y  R  G  H  W  U
P  T  O  L  G  F  E  A  C  E  Y
D  H  S  U  N  D  A  Y  F  D  D
I  U  W  J  S  D  D  P  A  N  S
S  R  M  T  W  T  F  S  P  E  X
S  S  J  F  M  A  M  F  B  S  C
Y  D  J  J  S  A  O  R  P  D  V
G  A  N  D  O  T  F  I  P  A  B
F  Y  F  T  U  E  S  D  A  Y  H
H  I  O  N  E  I  S  A  O  E  J
S  A  T  U  R  D  A  Y  G  L  P
J  M  P  Q  W  S  L  N  T  Y  D
U  E  R  L  H  T  Y  F  Y  J  A
X  I  L  W  R  V  A  O  W  P  M
```

Context Clues

One word has been highlighted in each sentence below. There are two definitions given for the word. Decide which meaning is correct by reading the sentence and thinking about how the word is used. Circle the correct meaning.

1. The **bail** was broken, so the bucket of water was difficult to lift.
   a. throw water out   **b.** the handle of a pail

2. The princess had a grand time at the **ball** last night.
   a. a dance   **b.** a round object

3. Joe **left** before I could tell him good-bye.
   a. the opposite of right   **b.** went away

4. Jack had a **fit** when his brother broke his new bicycle.
   a. suitable   **b.** an attack

5. The group became **grave** when they saw the danger they were in.
   a. serious   **b.** a place of burial

Three-Digit Addition

Time yourself. How fast can you complete the problems?

A.

410	737	426	166	404	259	272
+ 291	+ 288	+ 497	+ 617	+ 395	+ 450	+ 438

B.

357	519	834	313	558	687	901
+ 417	+ 170	+ 196	+ 488	+ 184	+ 139	+ 149

Time:

Number correct:

Reading a Bar Graph

The bar graph below shows how many boxes of cookies were
sold at Discovery Elementary School over an eight-week period.
Use the graph to answer the questions.

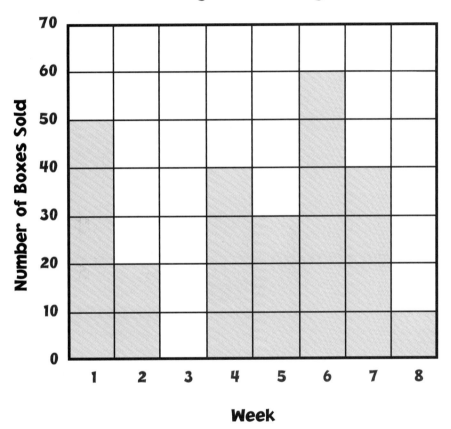

**Boxes of Cookies Sold at
Discovery Elementary School**

Week

A. What was the total number of boxes sold during the eight-week sale? _____

B. During which two weeks were the same number of boxes sold? _____

C. How many more boxes were sold during week 6 than week 7? _____

D. How many fewer boxes were sold during week 8 than week 2? _____

E. How many boxes were sold during week 3? _____ What do you think might

have happened? _____

Three-Digit Column Addition

Add to solve each problem.

A. 402
    715
  + 513

B. 800
    240
  + 912

C. 257
    946
  + 178

D. 589
    456
  + 981

E. 643
    285
    133
  + 341

F. 321
    419
    444
  + 750

G. 814
    901
    121
  + 215

H. 136
    912
    978
  + 222

Riddles

Twenty white horses up a red hill.
Now they chomp. Now they stomp.
Now they stand still.
What are they?

The words in the box make a riddle. They have a hidden meaning. Can you guess what the riddle is about? The answer is teeth! There are twenty white teeth in your mouth. The red hill is your gums. As you talk, they move up and down as if they are chomping and stomping. When you finish talking, they "stand still."

Riddles give a symbolic meaning to things. They have been used for thousands of years. In ancient times, wise people would often answer questions with riddles. It was believed that knowledge was precious, or of great value, and should not be given to everyone. If a person could solve a riddle, he was smart enough to know the answer.

1. What is the main idea of this story?
   a. Riddles are used as symbols.
   b. Riddles have been used for many years.
   c. Riddles are hard to figure out.

2. What is a riddle?_____

3. The word **precious** means:
   a. a lot of money
   b. meaning
   c. valuable

4. Instead of giving an answer, why did wise people speak in riddles?

_____

_____

34

Alphabetical Order

Write the months in **alphabetical order** on the lines.
Then, write the **abbreviation** beside each month. Circle the month of your birthday.

Word List

January	February	March	April	September	June
December	August	May	October	November	July

1. _____

2. _____

3. _____

4. _____

5. _____

6. _____

7. _____

8. _____

9. _____

10. _____

11. _____

12. _____

Word Problems

Solve each word problem.

A. Dexter made $5.00 washing cars on Monday, $2.75 on Tuesday, and $6.25 on Wednesday. How much money did Dexter make in the three days of car washing?

_____

B. Missy took 114 pictures last June, 121 last July, and 109 last August. How many pictures did Missy take last summer?

_____

C. Kerry ate two oranges at breakfast and half an orange at lunch. At dinner, Kerry ate the other half of the orange from lunch. How many oranges did Kerry eat?

_____

D. Sandy sold 65 books at the book sale on Thursday, 231 books on Friday, and 111 more on Saturday. How many books did Sandy sell in three days?

_____

Three-Digit Addition

Add to solve the problems.

A. 358
  + 227

B. 371
  + 389

C. 408
  + 159

D. 327
  + 196

E. 730
  + 197

F. 344
  + 523

G. 751
  + 225

H. 400
  +127

I. 111
  + 345

J. 250
  +178

K. 382
  + 160

L. 348
  + 436

M. 428
  + 150

N. 197
  + 402

O. 724
  + 150

P. 181
  + 199

Q. 451
  + 315

R. 613
  + 178

Cloze

Read the story below. Many words are missing.
Fill in the blanks with words from the word list.

Word List

danced
down
had
peeking
puddles
pulled
reached
red
stepped
Sure
was
weather
would

Hunting for a Rainbow

Maggie pulled the rubber boots on over her shoes. She slid into her yellow raincoat and _____ the front closed. This was just the _____ she had been hoping for. The sky _____ a light gray with bits of blue _____ through. Maggie knew that this time she _____ find what she was looking for. She _____ outside and opened the big, _____ umbrella over her head. The light rain _____ on the rounded top and quickly slid _____ the sides. Her boots splashed in the _____ as Maggie walked through them. The rain _____ almost stopped so Maggie hurried faster. She _____ the top of the hill and looked. _____ enough, this time she found it! Beyond the hill was a beautiful rainbow sparkling in the sun.

36

The Old Farmer and His Magic Bird

1

On his 80th birthday, something strange happened. As Arius was wandering in the forest looking for firewood, he fell over a fallen log. When he climbed back to his feet, the old man heard a wondrous sound unlike anything he'd ever heard. It was a song that sounded as if a hundred fairies were whistling to him.

He felt his way along the path toward the sound until he saw something on a branch in front of him. It was a tiny bird with wings of red and gold and a chest of blue and green. Arius had never seen anything so beautiful. Then, he remembered the storyteller's tale. He knew the bird must be the rainbow warbler.

The bird did not stop singing until the farmer snuck up on it and covered it with his cloak. Happily, Arius made his way out of the forest and headed home.

3

A long time ago, there was an old farmer named Arius who was very tired of living a hard life. His back ached and his hands were crooked from years of digging and planting. He lived alone on a tiny farm far away from the nearest kingdom, and no one ever visited him.

Every morning, he would wake before dawn and tend to his crops. His garden gave him barely enough food to eat, and there was never anything left to sell. At night, he would sit in his small hut and feel his heart grow heavy and sad.

When Arius was a boy, a mysterious storyteller once told him of a magical bird called a rainbow warbler. If captured, the bird would make its owner young and rich forever. Now that Arius was old and alone, there wasn't a day that passed that he didn't wish he could find that bird. More than anything in the world, he wanted another chance at life.

2

As soon as he reached his hut, Arius placed the bird in a small wire cage. Then, tired after his adventure, he plopped down on his cot and fell asleep.

When he awoke the next morning, his back wasn't hurting like it normally did. His hands and fingers were no longer crooked and swollen with pain. Something had happened to him. He looked in the mirror and saw a face 50 years younger staring back at him. The old farmer was a young man again!

Arius was so excited, he ran out the front door and tripped. When he got up to see what he'd stumbled over, he saw a small wooden chest. Removing the lid, he found that it was filled with hundreds of gold coins. Not only was Arius a young man, but he was a rich one, too. The storyteller's tale had come true!

4

As the days passed, the farmer grew even younger and a new chest of gold appeared on his doorstep each morning. One day, Arius ventured into the kingdom and bought a huge new farm and all of the things he ever wanted.

Wherever he went, he took the bird with him in its cage. He did not want to risk losing it. But as time went by, he started to notice that the beautiful creature seemed to be growing sadder. It never sang the beautiful song he'd heard in the forest. It never tried to fly or flutter its wings. Even its radiant colors were beginning to fade.

Arius also noticed that even though his body was getting younger and he had all the wealth he could want, his heart was still heavy and sad. Everything in his new garden dried up and stopped growing. Arius had youth but no one to share it with, because he avoided other people. He feared that they might try to steal the warbler from him if they learned its secret. So he sat alone every night in front of the fire with no one to talk to and nothing to do.

5

The days passed and soon Arius's youth faded away. Once again, he had the body of an 80-year-old man with a bent back and crooked hands. But somehow, it didn't matter to him. He felt better now that he knew the rainbow warbler was free. He moved back to his old farm and gave away all the things he'd bought with the chests of gold.

Then, one morning, as he was planting seeds in his garden, he heard a familiar noise. It was the sound of a hundred fairies whistling softly. He looked up in the sky, and there, circling above him, was the warbler with its beautiful colors restored. It had returned to him.

7

Then, one day, Arius discovered that the rainbow warbler had lost all of its color. It was now just a gray bird that did not sing. He was afraid that the bird might die. Somehow, that did not seem fair to Arius, and it made him sad to think about it. Why should such a beautiful creature be sacrificed just so he could look better in the mirror?

Arius took the cage outside, and, with a brief sigh, opened its door. Slowly, the bird hobbled out and flapped its wings. It looked at Arius for a moment and then flew off into the trees. The farmer watched it go and sadly waved good-bye.

6

Arius soon learned that there had been no need to keep the bird in a cage. It never left his side now that it was free, and although Arius did not have the body of a young man, his heart grew lighter and happier.

Every day, he awoke to the bird's gentle song. His garden blossomed and people came from miles around to buy the wonderful fruits and vegetables that he now grew. He was never lonely again, as he and the rainbow warbler lived together happily ever after.

8

Antonym Search

Match each pair of antonyms by connecting a word from the first column of the word list with a word from the second column. Then, find and circle each antonym pair in the word search. (Hint: Each pair of words is spelled across and down and shares one letter.) One pair has already been done for you.

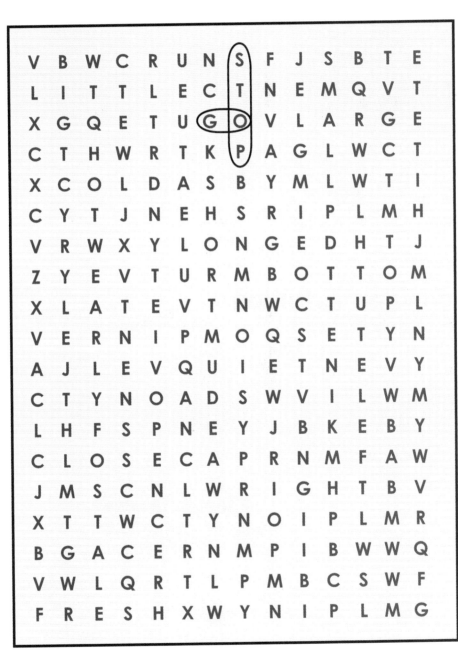

Word List

left	little
big	right
small	late
early	close
open	large
fresh	go
stop	long
short	stale
hot	bottom
noisy	quiet
top	cold

Can You Spell?

Underline the **spelling error** in each sentence.
Write the **correct spelling** of the word on the line.

1. Are you goeing to the ball game?

2. My room is very cleen.

3. Ronnie baught some gum at the store.

4. Tony payed $15.00 to get his bike fixed.

5. Pepper makes Becky sneaze.

6. Billy loves ice creem.

7. Travis is very frendly.

Math

Column Addition

Add to find the sums. Regroup if needed.

A.	33	B.	20	C.	23	D.	36
	45		37		14		25
	16		41		21		57
	21		19		26		19
	+ 25		+ 402		+ 382		+ 503

E.	456	F.	632	G.	254	H.	636
	219		169		513		258
	+ 387		+ 402		+ 382		+ 503

Alphabetical Order

Write the words from the word list in **alphabetical order** on the lines.

1. _____

2. _____

3. _____

4. _____

5. _____

6. _____

7. _____

8. _____

9. _____

10. _____

11. _____

12. _____

13. _____

14. _____

15. _____

16. _____

Word List

Mars	Venus
Mercury	Jupiter
Uranus	Neptune
satellite	universe
planet	shuttle
Earth	asteroid
Saturn	Pluto
moon	astronauts

Types of Sentences

Read each sentence. Using the key, write the corresponding letter on the line to name the sentence type. Then, write the correct **punctuation** at the end of the sentence.

_____ 1. Carol lives in a pretty house ☐

_____ 2. Does Joyce like peanut butter ☐

_____ 3. We miss Terry very much ☐

_____ 4. Take Timmy's cat to his house ☐

_____ 5. Wow, Kenneth hit a home run ☐

_____ 6. Ouch, that hurt ☐

Key

C = Command
E = Exclamation
S = Statement
Q = Question

Write an example of each of the following types of sentences.

Command _____

_____

Exclamation _____

_____

Question _____

_____

Statement _____

_____

Compound Words

Write a word from the word list on each line to form a **compound word.**
Find each compound word in the word search at the bottom of the page.

Word List

work	brush	noon	foot	ball	board
burger	stick	fall	corn	mark	bell

after _____

bare _____

book_____

cheese _____

water _____

pop_____

tooth_____

skate _____

candle_____

base_____

home _____

door _____

```
F  B  B  C  S  J  H  O  M  E  W  O  R  K  K
M  A  O  D  H  K  J  J  L  X  W  J  J  C  X
J  S  O  O  H  E  D  N  K  K  U  F  I  I  M
X  E  K  O  P  E  E  C  C  X  S  T  Y  R  D
B  B  M  R  Y  B  M  S  R  G  S  I  L  F  P
A  A  A  B  Y  S  C  L  E  E  F  Z  T  U  O
R  L  R  E  Y  M  R  N  L  B  Y  F  A  E  P
E  L  K  L  J  B  J  D  W  I  U  O  K  E  C
F  A  D  L  M  S  N  H  Z  I  V  R  J  T  O
O  A  C  P  R  A  B  E  I  W  A  B  G  Q  R
O  P  T  R  C  S  C  F  A  L  M  M  H  E  N
T  R  F  D  M  W  A  T  E  R  F  A  L  L  R
S  K  A  T  E  B  O  A  R  D  M  S  O  C  C
X  U  Z  M  M  T  O  O  T  H  B  R  U  S  H
A  F  T  E  R  N  O  O  N  J  H  T  V  P  S
```

Building Vocabulary

Beth wants to be a paramedic and she practices on her dog, Gumbo. Read the story to see how Gumbo feels about all of this. Then, read each of the five sentences. Write the letter for the best answer on the line.

Good Old Gumbo . . .

No dog was ever as patient as Gumbo. Just ask Beth. She is his owner. Beth has put Gumbo through a great deal in his young life. He's been a model for **assorted** doll clothes. He's **retrieved** baseballs from under thick hedges. Now Gumbo is a model again. This time it's for splints and bandages.

Beth is learning all about first aid. She hopes to be a paramedic one day. She thinks helping people would be a good thing. She wants to practice every bandage and splint on Gumbo.

After only five minutes, Gumbo has become **disturbed**. He doesn't think being wrapped up is much fun. He decides that he'd better do something **immediately**. He has heard the saying, "being all tied up." Gumbo wants to get out of this while he still can!

_____ 1. The word **assorted** means:
    a. tired   **b.** mixed   **c.** hungry   **d.** distant

_____ 2. The word **retrieved** means:
    a. bought   **b.** made   **c.** begged   **d.** brought back

_____ 3. The word **disturbed** means:
    a. upset   **b.** soft   **c.** silly   **d.** loud

_____ 4. The word **immediately** means:
    a. now   **b.** inside   **c.** under   **d.** never

_____ 5. A word in the story that is a synonym of **bound** is:
    a. owner   **b.** learning   **c.** tied   **d.** wrapped

Practice New Words

On a separate sheet of paper, write one sentence using each of these words:

assorted   retrieved   disturbed   immediately

Main Idea

The **main idea** of a paragraph is its central thought or topic. Read each paragraph. Read the three phrases under each paragraph. Decide which one tells the main idea. Write the letter of that phrase on the line.

_____ **1.**   Gary and Fritz have been writing to each other for four years. Gary lives in Indiana and Fritz lives in Germany. Gary looks forward to Fritz's letters. Fritz usually sends at least one picture and sometimes he sends extra German stamps for Gary's collection. Gary and Fritz both hope that they can meet someday. They feel as if they know each other already.

    a. Pictures from Germany   **b.** Gary's German pen pal   **c.** Gary's friend

_____ **2.**   Mary has been blind all of her life. She has gone to special schools to learn to do things for herself. Her best friend Katy is not blind. Katy and Mary help each other. Mary is trying to teach Katy to read Braille. It is a special system of raised dots that lets Mary "read" the page. Katy isn't doing very well at all. Katy says that it is hard for her to "see" the letters with her fingers.

    a. Learning to read   **b.** Understanding Braille   **c.** A special friendship

What's Missing?

Print the correct number in the box to complete each number sentence.

A. $2 + \boxed{} = 13$ **B.** $38 - \boxed{} = 24$ **C.** $28 - \boxed{} = 15$

D. $73 + \boxed{} = 89$ **E.** $40 - \boxed{} = 33$ **F.** $82 + \boxed{} = 97$

G. $55 + \boxed{} = 73$ **H.** $56 - \boxed{} = 13$ **I.** $19 + \boxed{} = 33$

J. $26 + \boxed{} = 35$ **K.** $28 - \boxed{} = 19$ **L.** $77 - \boxed{} = 59$

Two-Digit Subtraction Review

Calculate the following **subtraction** problems. Regroup as needed.

A. 15
   – 5

B. 25
   – 3

C. 10
   – 2

D. 19
   – 5

E. 14
   – 5

F. 16
   – 4

G. 19
   – 2

H. 21
   – 7

I. 40
   – 5

J. 62
   – 9

K. 28
   – 16

L. 38
   – 12

M. 42
   – 7

N. 46
   – 25

O. 28
   – 14

Analogies

Fill in the blanks to complete the **analogies**.

1. A **mouth** is to **taste** as an **eye** is to _____ .

2. A **person** is to a **house** as a **bear** is to a _____ .

3. An **apple** is to a **tree** as a **watermelon** is to a _____ .

4. A **kitten** is to a **cat** as a **puppy** is to a _____ .

5. An **inch** is to **length** as a **pound** is to _____ .

6. A **car** is to a **road** as a **boat** is to _____ .

7. A **whale** is to **water** as an **elephant** is to _____ .

Nouns and Verbs

Read each sentence below. Underline each **noun**. Circle each **verb**.

1. Ryan and Cathy went to the museum.

2. Beverly washes the big, green car.

3. The big, black dog scared Chris.

4. Wanda lives in Georgia.

5. Don owns a large store.

6. The warm night was peaceful.

7. The girl was late for practice.

8. Brian put the blue sweater in the dryer.

9. Amber had fun at the park.

Regroup or Not to Regroup?

Subtract to find each difference.

A. 63 − 21	B. 45 − 25	C. 75 − 23	D. 33 − 11	E. 46 − 21
F. 32 − 15	G. 55 − 27	H. 90 − 42	I. 75 − 68	J. 35 − 16

49

Building Vocabulary

Davey has a new friend who keeps bothering him. Read the story to find out more. Then, read each of the five sentences. Write the letter for the best answer on the line.

A Fishing Friend

It all began last summer when Davey was fishing at his grandpa's farm. Suddenly, something odd **occurred**. A big head **emerged** from the water. Davey was **terrified** at first. The creature smiled and told Davey that his name was Clarence.

Clarence told Davey that he had always been alone and was tired of his **solitude**. He wanted a friend. Davey felt sorry for Clarence and tried his best to cheer him up.

Now it seems that Davey has a friend for life. There's just one problem: Clarence wants to be with Davey all the time. Davey can't go fishing alone anymore. He hopes Clarence will find another new friend soon. Davey would like some of his own solitude. He would also like to catch some fish. Few fish come around when Clarence is near!

_____ 1. The word **occurred** means:
    a. pointed   **b.** painted   **c.** scraped   **d.** happened

_____ 2. The word **emerged** means:
    a. fell in   **b.** came out   **c.** divided   **d.** twisted around

_____ 3. The word **terrified** means:
    a. scared   **b.** rich   **c.** healthy   **d.** ripped

_____ 4. The word **solitude** means:
    a. teacher   **b.** friends   **c.** leaving   **d.** being alone

_____ 5. A word in the story that is a synonym for **desired** is:
    a. wanted   **b.** problem   **c.** cheer   **d.** destroyed

Practice New Words

On a separate sheet of paper, write one sentence using each of these words:

occurred   **emerged**   **terrified**   **solitude**

Beat the Clock (Double-Digit Subtraction)

Make several copies of this page. Time yourself every day for a week.
Does your time improve? Does your accuracy increase?

A.

$$
\begin{array}{r} 86 \\ -58 \\ \hline \end{array}
\qquad
\begin{array}{r} 90 \\ -29 \\ \hline \end{array}
\qquad
\begin{array}{r} 42 \\ -28 \\ \hline \end{array}
\qquad
\begin{array}{r} 94 \\ -66 \\ \hline \end{array}
\qquad
\begin{array}{r} 62 \\ -49 \\ \hline \end{array}
\qquad
\begin{array}{r} 55 \\ -17 \\ \hline \end{array}
\qquad
\begin{array}{r} 41 \\ -25 \\ \hline \end{array}
$$

B.

$$
\begin{array}{r} 75 \\ -17 \\ \hline \end{array}
\qquad
\begin{array}{r} 47 \\ -18 \\ \hline \end{array}
\qquad
\begin{array}{r} 40 \\ -29 \\ \hline \end{array}
\qquad
\begin{array}{r} 61 \\ -23 \\ \hline \end{array}
\qquad
\begin{array}{r} 54 \\ -38 \\ \hline \end{array}
\qquad
\begin{array}{r} 81 \\ -27 \\ \hline \end{array}
\qquad
\begin{array}{r} 67 \\ -38 \\ \hline \end{array}
$$

C.

$$
\begin{array}{r} 91 \\ -56 \\ \hline \end{array}
\qquad
\begin{array}{r} 52 \\ -49 \\ \hline \end{array}
\qquad
\begin{array}{r} 43 \\ -38 \\ \hline \end{array}
\qquad
\begin{array}{r} 71 \\ -34 \\ \hline \end{array}
\qquad
\begin{array}{r} 75 \\ -46 \\ \hline \end{array}
\qquad
\begin{array}{r} 84 \\ -47 \\ \hline \end{array}
\qquad
\begin{array}{r} 61 \\ -12 \\ \hline \end{array}
$$

D.

$$
\begin{array}{r} 93 \\ -75 \\ \hline \end{array}
\qquad
\begin{array}{r} 84 \\ -19 \\ \hline \end{array}
\qquad
\begin{array}{r} 82 \\ -73 \\ \hline \end{array}
\qquad
\begin{array}{r} 84 \\ -37 \\ \hline \end{array}
\qquad
\begin{array}{r} 66 \\ -48 \\ \hline \end{array}
\qquad
\begin{array}{r} 75 \\ -27 \\ \hline \end{array}
\qquad
\begin{array}{r} 54 \\ -39 \\ \hline \end{array}
$$

E.

$$
\begin{array}{r} 87 \\ -38 \\ \hline \end{array}
\qquad
\begin{array}{r} 74 \\ -25 \\ \hline \end{array}
\qquad
\begin{array}{r} 67 \\ -38 \\ \hline \end{array}
\qquad
\begin{array}{r} 71 \\ -64 \\ \hline \end{array}
\qquad
\begin{array}{r} 83 \\ -28 \\ \hline \end{array}
\qquad
\begin{array}{r} 41 \\ -34 \\ \hline \end{array}
\qquad
\begin{array}{r} 71 \\ -42 \\ \hline \end{array}
$$

Time:

Number correct:

More Nouns and Verbs

Look at the words in the word list.
Write the **nouns** on the building.
Write the **verbs** on the rocket.

Word List

pretend
news
remove
school
cow
be
earth
flee
sell
lamp
car
took
speak
hear
berry
lake
bring
heart
window
understand
easel
wear

Plurals (-s or -es)

Add the correct ending (**s** or **es**) to make each word **plural**.
Write the new words on the lines.

1. teacher _____

2. potato _____

3. house _____

4. kite _____

5. class _____

6. clown _____

7. box _____

8. handbook _____

9. watch _____

10. friend _____

11. clock _____

12. computer _____

13. couch _____

14. carmel _____

15. fox _____

Adding & Subtracting with Decimals

Add or **subtract** to solve each problem.

A. 7.0
  + 7.5

B. 9.2
  − 4.1

C. 8.3
  + 2.8

D. 23.5
  − 16.3

E. 4.23
  + 1.95

F. 6.35
  − 4.96

G. 2.98
  + 6.85

H. 96.3
  − 21.4

I. 6.91
  + 2.98

Story Problems

Solve each word problem.

A. Shannon bought 3 dozen eggs at the store. On the way home, she dropped the egg cartons and 13 of the eggs broke. How many unbroken eggs does Shannon now have? _____

B. Dawn is allowed to swim in the pool for 60 minutes each day. If she has been swimming today for 25 minutes, how many more minutes does she have left in the pool? _____

C. There were 937 students at Ridge Hill School. If 43 students missed school due to illness, how many students were at school? _____

D. Phil's Used Car Lot had 142 cars to sell. If Phil sold 26 of the cars, how many did he have left to sell? _____

E. Together, Cindy and Jim counted 221 cars on their road trip. Cindy counted 132 of the cars. How many cars did Jim count? _____

Categories

Read each group of words or phrases. Choose the best category name from the box. Write the correct category under each list. The first one has been done for you.

Categories:
types of berries	summer clothing
things during a storm	baby animals
~~yellow things~~	

1.
A. sun
B. banana
C. daisy
D. corn
E. lemon

Category:

yellow things

2.
A. bathing suit
B. sunglasses
C. shorts
D. sandals
E. short-sleeved shirt

Category:

_____

3.
A. strawberry
B. raspberry
C. blackberry
D. blueberry
E. boysenberry

Category:

_____

4.
A. foal
B. lamb
C. chick
D. duckling
E. kitten

Category:

_____

Possessive Plurals

Make each highlighted word **possessive** by rewriting the word on the line and adding an apostrophe in the correct place.

1. That is **Danas** dollhouse. _____

2. **Craigs** truck is very big. _____

3. I like **Sharons** new green bicycle. _____

4. The **childrens** song was perfectly in tune. _____

5. The two **girls** kites flew high in the sky. _____

6. The **schools** end-of-the-year picnic was fun. _____

7. The **trucks** loud horn scared Barbara. _____

8. The **actors** costume was colorful. _____

9. I love to visit my **grandmothers** house. _____

10. The **singers** voices are beautiful. _____

11. Those **dogs** collars are green. _____

Three- and Four-Digit Subtraction

Subtract to solve each problem. Circle the smallest answer.
Draw a square around the largest answer.

A. 912
    − 735

B. 583
    − 321

C. 185
    − 112

D. 635
    − 504

E. 865
    − 125

F. 999
    − 428

G. 2,190
    − 1,065

H. 5,948
    − 2,374

Three-Digit Subtraction

Subtract to solve each problem. Circle all of the even numbers.

A.

423	222	435	628	757	637	423
− 285	− 153	− 166	− 499	− 178	− 388	− 285

B.

326	972	685	518	741	438	371
− 285	− 609	− 246	− 329	− 362	− 258	− 283

C.

529	625	514	664	742	200	634
− 482	− 407	− 126	− 278	− 467	− 158	− 277

Adjectives

Underline the **adjectives** in each paragraph below.
The first adjective has been underlined for you.

1.   I like <u>chocolate</u> ice cream. Chocolate ice cream tastes good when it is hot outside. Unfortunately, chocolate ice cream makes a big, sticky mess. I solve this problem by eating my yummy, chocolate ice cream outside.

2.   One sunny day, I found a white rabbit hopping in front of my house. I walked up to the frightened rabbit and talked to him. He finally calmed down and I picked him up. His soft fur tickled my hands. I took the sweet rabbit behind my house to the big forest. Waiting there for him was his happy mother. The two small rabbits hopped home together.

Persuasive Paragraph

You must convince your mom to let you go bowling.
Ask her, give your reasons, and then ask again.

Title of paragraph: _____

Question: May I _____

Reasons:

1. _____

2. _____

3. _____

4. _____

Ask again: _____

Use the information above to write a paragraph. Ask the question. State the reasons, and then ask the question again. Indent the first sentence. Use capital letters and periods. Remember to give your paragraph a title.

_____

_____

_____

_____

_____

_____

_____

_____

Abbreviations

Write the correct **abbreviation** for each word on the line next to it.
Use a dictionary to check your answers for spelling and capitalization.

Street _____   pound _____   minute _____

Junior _____   ounce _____   foot _____

Mister _____   Senior _____   inch _____

Doctor _____   centimeter _____   President _____

Apartment _____   Road _____   Mountain _____

Math

Subtraction Review

Subtract to solve each problem.

A.
```
  623        900        722        377        871        628
- 194      - 309      - 317      - 186      - 384      - 300
```

B.
```
  990        818        572        951        825        771
- 731      - 693      - 335      - 357      - 469      - 217
```

Write the answers in order from smallest to largest.

_____   _____   _____   _____   _____

_____   _____   _____   _____   _____

Subtraction with Decimals

Subtract to solve each problem.

A.
$$20.20$$
$$- 13.75$$

B.
$$334.5$$
$$- 145.6$$

C.
$$7.051$$
$$- 2.058$$

D.
$$3.812$$
$$- 2.116$$

E.
$$8.229$$
$$- 2.443$$

F.
$$421.6$$
$$- 334.7$$

Contractions

Read each sentence. Circle the correct **contraction** for the highlighted words.

1. I **did not** look at the movie when it was scary!   didn't   did'nt   don't

2. **You are** my best friend!   You'd   You'll   You're

3. Are you sure **we are** on the right path?   we'd   we'll   we're

4. Brian said **he is** older than you.   he'd   he's   he'll

5. **Who would** want to live in that dusty old house?   Who'd   Who's   Who've

6. **They are** very kind people.   They'll   They're   They've

7. **Let us** begin the lesson.   Lets   Let's   Lets'

8. **You are** going to be late for school.   Your'e   You're   Your

9. **You have** given me plenty of reasons to study.   You'd   You're   You've

10. **I am** going to the zoo tomorrow.   I'd   I'll   I'm

Pronouns

Read each sentence. Replace the highlighted word(s)
with the correct pronoun by writing it on the lines.

1. **Jim and Carla** like to ride motorcycles. _____ ride whenever they can.

2. **Jane** has two lovebirds. _____ sings to them every day.

3. **Chelsea and Cheyna** are sisters. Let's go to their house and play with _____.

4. **Billy** is a police officer. _____ likes to help people.

5. **This book** is from my grandparents. _____ is my favorite.

6. **Daphne and I** like jelly beans. _____ like to eat the red ones.

7. That is **Rocky's** baseball. Please give it to _____.

Subtraction with Decimals

A.   8.5
   − 2.8

B.   9.2
   − 7.5

C.   7.1
   − 4.1

D.   3.75
   − 2.12

E.   54.3
   − 19.4

F.   9.35
   − 5.68

G.   2.01
   − 1.95

H.   5.12
   − 4.08

I.   53.0
   − 22.6

If the answers were dollar amounts, which problem would you like?

Building Vocabulary

Ike and Spike are two young boys. Read the story to find out some of the messes they get themselves involved in. Then, read each of the five sentences. Write the letter for the best answer on the line.

Ike, Spike, and the Circle Game

Ike and Spike are two brave little boys who will try anything once. There's just one problem. These nine-year-old friends can never agree. They always want to do things in different ways. That's quite a **dilemma** sometimes!

Once they **created** a large mural. Ike's faces were smiling, and Spike's faces all frowned. Another day, the boys went for a long hike. Ike took the path up into the hills, and Spike walked down by the river. They didn't find each other again until the next day.

Here you see them **struggling** to get home from a fishing **excursion**. Each boy wants to go a different way. These poor guys have been spinning in circles for an hour. Maybe soon one will get tired so they can at least move the boat!

_____ 1. The word **dilemma** means:
   a. canoe   b. problem   c. bait   d. song

_____ 2. The word **created** means:
   a. made   b. heard   c. told   d. found

_____ 3. The word **struggling** means:
   a. laughing   b. running   c. trying hard   d. painting

_____ 4. The word **excursion** means:
   a. hat   b. lesson   c. trip   d. fort

_____ 5. A word in the story that is a synonym for **varied** is:
   a. ordinary   b. poor   c. problem   d. different

Practice New Words

On a separate sheet of paper, write one sentence using each of these words:

dilemma   created   struggling   excursion

Mixed Problems with Decimals

Add or **subtract** to solve each problem.

List the answers from largest to smallest.

A. 726.6
  + 122.5

B. 9.025
  – 1.874

C. 423.8
  + 111.4

D. 8.345
  + 2.137

E. 77.61
  – 44.32

F. 522.7
  + 311.7

_____

_____

_____

_____

_____

_____

Using Guide Words

Look at the words in the word list. Print each word in alphabetical order below the two **guide words** it would appear between in a dictionary.

Word List

1. aardvark   afghan

2. Africa   aim

aggravate
above
aboard
affect
about
after
aid
agree
ailment
afford

Understanding What I've Read

Parasites

Some animals get their food by living in or on other things. These animals, called parasites, do not kill the animals they live on, but they may harm or irritate them. A flea will live on a dog, cat, or other animals. The animal it lives on is called the host. The flea gets its food by sucking the other animal's blood. The flea will not harm the host, but it will make the host itch and feel uncomfortable. Some worms are also parasites. A tapeworm lives inside the body of an animal. It eats the food the host has eaten. The tapeworm can make the host very sick. Plants can be parasites, too. Mistletoe and some types of ferns live on trees, taking food and water from them.

1. What is the main idea of this story?
   a. Parasites live on or in other living things.
   b. A flea is a parasite.
   c. Parasites can make their hosts sick.

2. How does a flea get food?
   _____

3. Where does a tapeworm live?
   _____

4. What is a parasite? _____

   _____

5. What does the word **host** mean?
   a. an animal that lives on another living thing
   b. the animal a parasite lives on
   c. mistletoe

6. What kinds of plants can be parasites?

   _____

Beat the Clock (Multiplication Facts 0 to 9)

A.

7	4	3	9	1	8	2	6	0	5
x 4	x 6	x 1	x 5	x 4	x 4	x 3	x 8	x 6	x 5

B.

8	4	0	4	3	6	7	1	8	2
x 1	x 0	x 3	x 3	x 5	x 3	x 3	x 0	x 9	x 7

C.

5	2	8	0	5	4	1	9	3	6
x 4	x 0	x 7	x 0	x 1	x 7	x 6	x 1	x 8	x 0

D.

7	4	2	6	9	0	5	7	1	3
x 1	x 9	x 4	x 7	x 0	x 7	x 9	x 6	x 3	x 4

E.

0	8	3	5	1	9	5	2	6	4
x 9	x 5	x 2	x 6	x 1	x 4	x 0	x 2	x 2	x 5

F.

7	3	1	8	6	4	2	8	0	5
x 7	x 9	x 5	x 0	x 6	x 1	x 6	x 3	x 2	x 2

G.

9	1	7	4	0	5	9	2	8	3
x 3	x 9	x 0	x 4	x 5	x 8	x 9	x 1	x 8	x 0

H.

2	6	6	1	7	4	0	9	3	7
x 8	x 1	x 9	x 7	x 5	x 8	x 1	x 8	x 7	x 9

I.

5	0	6	3	5	2	8	7	1	9
x 7	x 8	x 4	x 3	x 3	x 9	x 6	x 2	x 2	x 7

J.

8	3	0	7	2	9	1	9	4	6
x 2	x 6	x 4	x 8	x 5	x 2	x 8	x 6	x 2	x 5

Time: _____   **Number correct:** _____

The Monster's Footprints

1

He led her across the street to the field by Oscar Sampson's farm. Tim's older sister, Alice, was standing by the fence, staring out into space.

"Hi, Alice," Kelly said. "What are you looking at?"

Alice pointed at the field. "Do you see them?" she asked.

Kelly shook her head, but then she noticed three sets of tracks in the snow heading across the field toward the barn. The tracks in the center were much larger than the other two.

Kelly shrugged. "So? What's so unusual about tracks in the snow?"

"Look closer," Tim replied.

3

It seemed like Kelly Hoover's lucky day. An unexpected snowstorm the night before had closed school for the day. She wolfed down her breakfast, put on her coat and boots, and was outside before the clock struck eight.

Her little neighbor Tim was already waiting for her in the front yard. He was a pest, but Tim's father was a refrigerator salesman, and the cardboard boxes he brought home were fun to build forts with—especially snow forts. So Kelly was happy to see him.

But Tim had something else in mind. "You've got to see this!" he exclaimed as soon as she stepped out the door. "Follow me!"

2

Kelly climbed over the fence and examined the tracks. She noticed that the two small ones were boot prints.

"Those were ours," Alice pointed out.

The tracks in the center looked like giant bare footprints with toes as big as soda cans.

"They go all the way up to Mr. Sampson's barn," said Tim. "Then, they stop and reappear on the other side, like whatever it was just walked through solid walls."

"Then where do they go?" Kelly asked.

"To Mr. Sampson's house, and then they stop. Do you think he's a monster? Or a ghost? Maybe, the Abdominal Snowman or something?"

Kelly frowned. "You mean Abominable. And no, I don't think Mr. Sampson's a monster. That's goofy."

"But he's so mean!" Alice exclaimed. "Once he yelled at us for petting his dog."

"That's because Sniffer's dangerous. He bites," Kelly replied.

"Still, he didn't have to yell."

4

Prefixes

Use the prefix bank and word list to **create as many words as you can**.
Write the words on the lines. Use another sheet of paper if needed.

Prefix Bank

dis- in- pre- re- un-

Word List

able	dent
form	charge
close	qualify
fill	related
civilized	sole
miss	pay
capable	heat
come	cover
wind	view

1. _____
2. _____
3. _____
4. _____
5. _____
6. _____
7. _____
8. _____
9. _____
10. _____
11. _____
12. _____
13. _____
14. _____
15. _____
16. _____
17. _____
18. _____
19. _____
20. _____
21. _____
22. _____

How Many?

Multiply. Circle all the **odd** answers.

A.

11	7	10	12	5	9	12
x 6	x 8	x 6	x 6	x 9	x 4	x 5

B.

10	9	11	3	8	10	7
x 4	x 3	x 7	x 8	x 8	x 2	x 9

C.

11	10	2	8	10	11	10
x 2	x 9	x 9	x 5	x 1	x 9	x 7

Building Vocabulary

Gordy the gorilla and Tussie the elephant are good friends. Read the story to learn more about one of their adventures. Then, read each of the five sentences. Write the letter for the best answer on the line.

Friends to the End

Tussie and Gordy are the best of friends. After all, they are the two largest and loudest creatures in the jungle. There was a time when they feared each other. Now they find that they can **actually** help each other. Sometimes Gordy will scrub Tussie's huge, gray back. Tussie returns the **favor** by making her trunk into a shower for Gordy.

Once they **combined** efforts to do something quite **noble**. A newborn tiger cub had wandered into the jungle. The cub's parents were worried and came to Gordy and Tussie for help. Tussie made big, wide paths through the thick jungle. Gordy swung from tree to tree looking everywhere. Together, in an hour's time, they found the tiger cub. Everyone was pleased!

_____ 1. The word **actually** means:
  a. slowly   **b.** hotly   **c.** angrily   **d.** really

_____ 2. The word **favor** means:
  a. drink   **b.** good deed   **c.** surprise   **d.** dark night

_____ 3. The word **combined** means:
  a. pointed   **b.** slid   **c.** joined   **d.** yelled

_____ 4. The word **noble** means:
  a. furry   **b.** good   **c.** calm   **d.** bad

_____ 5. A word in the story that is a synonym for **searching** is:
  a. scrubbing   **b.** worried   **c.** looking   **d.** pleasing

Practice New Words

On a separate sheet of paper, write one sentence using each of these words:

actually   favor   combined   noble

Find the Missing Factors

Write the missing **factor** to complete each fact.

A. 4 x ☐ = 12   ☐ x 5 = 0   8 x ☐ = 40

B. ☐ x 3 = 24   3 x ☐ = 27   ☐ x 9 = 63

C. 5 x ☐ = 35   ☐ x 1 = 18   9 x ☐ = 18

D. 6 x ☐ = 36   ☐ x 6 = 30   ☐ x 9 = 45

Homonyms

Read each sentence below.
Circle the **homonym** that completes each sentence correctly.

1. While in the woods, Kristen saw a (**bear   bare**).

2. Candy fell and hurt her (**tow   toe**).

3. The (**sale   sail**) on the boat billowed in the wind.

4. Sherry did not feel well and looked (**pail   pale**).

5. Teddy does not (**know   no**) how to play basketball.

6. We went to the mailbox and (**cent   sent**) a letter.

7. My cat had six kittens and four of them are (**mail   male**).

8. Sissy stopped to pick a (**flour   flower**) from the garden.

Multiplication Word Problems

Use **multiplication** to solve each word problem.

A. Stephen, Wendy, and Spencer each spent $9 at the amusement park. How much money did they spend altogether? $_____

B. Jennifer likes to make dolls. If she makes 3 dolls each day for 6 days, how many dolls will she have made? _____ **dolls**

C. Tory keeps his race cars in shoe boxes. He has 11 boxes with 5 cars in each. How many race cars does Tory have? _____ **race cars**

D. Tamika rode her bike for 2 hours every day for 8 days. How many hours did she ride altogether in those 8 days? _____ **hours**

E. Justin, Dylan, and Stephanie all wear hats. If they each have 12 hats, how many hats do they have altogether? _____ **hats**

F. Ursula had 3 mother cats. Each mother cat had 5 kittens. How many kittens did Ursula's cats have altogether? _____ **kittens**

G. Sean collects postage stamps. He puts 12 stamps on each page of his album. If Sean has 8 filled pages, how many stamps does Sean have? _____ **stamps**

H. Denise built 7 towers with building blocks. If she used 8 blocks for each tower, how many blocks did she use in all? _____ **blocks**

I. Gina wants to make friendship necklaces. She will use 9 beads on each necklace. How many beads does Gina need to make 5 necklaces? _____ **beads**

Compare and Contrast

Fill in the blanks to compare and contrast a newspaper and a book.
The first one has been done for you.

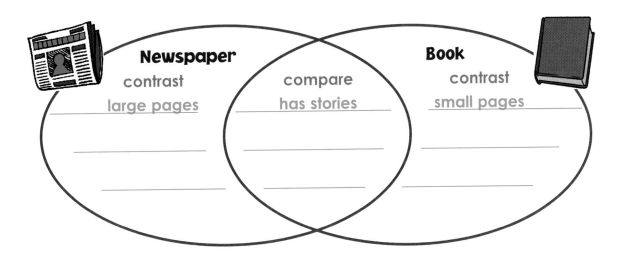

Newspaper
contrast
large pages
_____
_____

compare
has stories
_____
_____

Book
contrast
small pages
_____
_____

Write two paragraphs below. In the first paragraph, tell how newspapers
and books are alike. Tell how each is different in the second paragraph.
Be sure to indent the first sentence of each paragraph.

_____

_____

_____

_____

_____

_____

_____

_____

_____

Match the Fact to the Answer

4 x 5 =	8	1 x 5 =	24	6 x 3 =	40
2 x 7 =	18	5 x 3 =	5	0 x 9 =	6
8 x 1 =	20	3 x 8 =	12	1 x 7 =	0
9 x 2 =	15	2 x 6 =	21	8 x 5 =	18
5 x 3 =	14	7 x 3 =	15	6 x 1 =	7

Proper Nouns

Underline each **proper noun** in the story below. Write the correct capital letter above each proper noun. The first one has been done for you.

C

Last <u>christmas</u> mom, dad, billy, isabel, and I went to aunt mable and uncle buddy's house. All of our relatives were there having a good time. keisha, taylor, and maya all got new sneakers from santa claus. alex and kelli brought a pie for mrs. davis. The twins, dustin and dillon, showed off their new baby sister, stephanie. jamie brought her new doll. Everyone had a good time and looks forward to getting together on new year's day.

Understanding What I've Read

Space Probes

We learn about planets by observing, or studying, them. Scientists use telescopes to see planets. A telescope is a special instrument that makes faraway objects look bigger. Some planets are too far away to see clearly, even when we use a telescope. How can we learn about these planets? Scientists send special spacecraft called probes into space. Telescopes and cameras are sent in the probe to record everything they see. Probes also carry special instruments to examine the weather and soil on other planets. The information is sent back to Earth where scientists can study it. The first probe, called Mariner 2, was launched in 1962. It gave us information about the planet Venus. Since then, scientists have sent over 25 probes into space. Each probe tells us even more about other planets.

1. What is the main idea of this story?
   a. Probes tell us about other planets.
   b. Telescopes help us to see other planets.
   c. Mariner 2 was the first space probe.

2. What is a probe?

   _____

3. What information about other planets can a probe gather?

   _____

4. What does the word **observe** mean?
   a. a special instrument
   b. to study
   c. probe

5. What special equipment do probes carry?

   _____

A Multiplication Puzzle

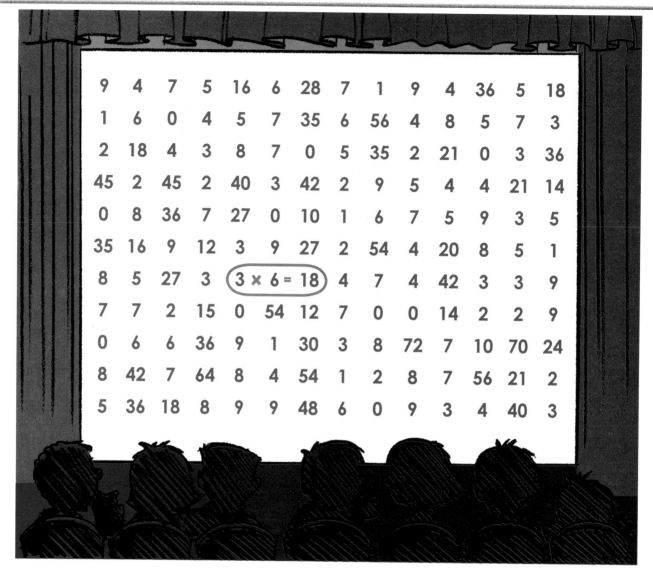

Problem List

Solve the problems on the list. Find each problem in the puzzle and fill in the **✗** and **=**. Circle the problems. One has been done for you.

3 x 6 = __18__	4 x 5 = _____
8 x 7 = _____	9 x 6 = _____
3 x 3 = _____	6 x 6 = _____
5 x 7 = _____	7 x 3 = _____
2 x 8 = _____	7 x 10 = _____
1 x 9 = _____	9 x 4 = _____
7 x 6 = _____	5 x 8 = _____

Descriptive Writing

The three adjectives below describe the picture. Add two more adjectives of your own. Write a paragraph about the picture using these adjectives. Remember to indent the first sentence of your paragraph and to include a title.

1. cheesy   2. messy   3. spicy

4. _____   5. _____

_____

_____

_____

_____

_____

Basic Facts

A.

0 x 4 = _____

1 x 9 = _____

5 x 7 = _____

3 x 4 = _____

2 x 9 = _____

7 x 6 = _____

B.

2 x 5 = _____

6 x 6 = _____

0 x 7 = _____

1 x 3 = _____

8 x 11 = _____

6 x 8 = _____

C.

8 x 0 = _____

4 x 10 = _____

2 x 1 = _____

8 x 8 = _____

9 x 6 = _____

5 x 6 = _____

Bonus: Circle the **even** answers.
Draw a square around the **odd** number answers.

One-Digit Times Two-Digit Multiplication

Multiply to solve the problems.

A.

21 x 9	70 x 0	42 x 3	76 x 6

B.

98 x 1	61 x 2	21 x 4	22 x 2

C.

64 x 4	29 x 5	38 x 7	56 x 9

Punctuation Review

Add the correct **punctuation** at the end of each sentence.

1. Who won the big football game _____

2. I went to the zoo last week with Tony _____

3. Please pass the salt _____

4. I would like to learn to sew _____

5. I cannot believe he did that _____

6. I can't get out of this tree. Help _____

7. Katie used to live in Texas _____

8. That ladder is going to fall. Look out _____

9. We are going to the lake _____

10. When is Elliott's birthday _____

Sequencing Events

Read the story to learn about the old house. Then, read the sentences below. Decide what happened first, second, and so on. Number the sentences in the correct order.

The Old House

Jerome was the one who discovered the old house in the first place. It was late one day last October. Jerome had taken a shortcut through the woods and there it was! That house was so spooky, it scared him just to look at it.

The next day at school, Jerome told Lisa Peterson. By the time the school day was through, the whole school knew about the house. All of the kids wanted to see it. A group of Jerome's friends planned to meet there right after dinner.

Nearly 20 boys and girls showed up at the house just before 6 o'clock. They walked around the old empty building in a close group.

Suddenly, they all heard a loud shriek. Everyone jumped and some children even screamed. Jerome looked up at one of the window ledges. There sat a big, black crow. All of the children laughed. They had let their imaginations get the best of them. They knew then that the house was not really scary. They all agreed that it had been a fun-filled adventure just the same.

_____ The children walked around the house.

_____ Jerome told Lisa Peterson about the house.

_____ The children knew the house was not scary.

_____ Jerome discovered the old house.

_____ The children saw a crow on a ledge.

_____ Nearly 20 boys and girls showed up at the old house before 6 o'clock.

_____ Some of Jerome's friends planned to meet at the old house after dinner.

One-Digit Times Three-Digit Multiplication

Multiply to solve the problems.

A. 173
    x 3

B. 452
    x 2

C. 168
    x 5

D. 223
    x 6

E. 180
    x 5

F. 232
    x 4

G. 549
    x 2

H. 257
    x 8

Write the answers in order from smallest to largest.

_____ _____ _____ _____

Combining Root Words and Suffixes

Use the suffix bank and the word list to **create as many words as you can**. Write the words on the lines at the bottom of the page. Remember to change the **y** to an **i** when adding a suffix. Use another sheet of paper if needed.

Suffix Bank

-er   -ful   -less
  -ly   -ness

Word List

teach	thought
beauty	boast
doubt	shy
happy	bake
sad	care
quick	friend
awkward	help
peace	law
quiet	wonder

1. _____
2. _____
3. _____
4. _____
5. _____
6. _____
7. _____
8. _____
9. _____
10. _____
11. _____
12. _____
13. _____
14. _____
15. _____
16. _____
17. _____
18. _____
19. _____
20. _____
21. _____
22. _____

Compound Words

Fill in each blank with a word from the word list to make a **compound word**.
Use each word only once.

Word List

boat	shore	case	fly	nap	bug
board	burger	crow	coat	book	time

scare_____

cook_____

cat_____

steam_____

suit_____

rain_____

night_____

cheese_____

sea_____

horse_____

chalk_____

lady_____

Story Problems

Solve each word problem.

A. The Super Coaster roller coaster ride has 15 cars. Each car has 4 seats. How many people can ride the Super Coaster at one time?

_____

B. Last week, 21 mother dogs had puppies. If they each had 6 puppies, how many puppies did the dogs have altogether? _____

C. Cheri can make 32 bracelets a week. She made bracelets for 12 weeks. How many bracelets did Cheri make? _____

D. Sixteen packages of crayons were donated to Mr. Horowitz's class. Each package had 64 crayons. How many crayons were donated in all?

_____

Greater Than or Less Than?

Multiply to solve the problems. Write **>** or **<** in the box to show if the first answer is greater or less than the second answer.

A.

159
x 8

☐

221
x 5

B.

983
x 3

☐

759
x 4

C.

865
x 1

☐

182
x 7

D.

135
x 9

☐

203
x 5

E.

315
x 4

☐

275
x 6

F.

249
x 2

☐

259
x 3

Using Synonyms

Read each sentence. Replace the word in parentheses with a **synonym**. Write the synonym on the line.

1. Rascal is a (small) _____ dog.

2. Timmy can run (fast) _____.

3. Did you (complete) _____ your homework?

4. I like to (yell) _____ when I am outside.

5. That box is an (odd) _____ color.

6. Will your mother (allow) _____ us to eat pizza?

7. My father brought me a (present) _____.

8. Kelly is wearing a (pretty) _____ dress.

9. Sonja recycled her (ancient) _____ letters.

10. The cat slept (below) _____ the table.

11. Patty likes to (converse) _____ with her friends.

The Steel-Drivin' Man

1

It was called the race of the century—the 19th century, that is. It was a contest of man versus machine, and when it was over, everyone knew the name of Big John Henry.

Back in the days before automobiles and airplanes, before machines did the work of men and women, Big John worked on the railroads in West Virginia, clearing the way for locomotives to steam across the Appalachian Mountains, moving people and goods from coast to coast.

3

John was the biggest, fastest, and strongest man working on the rails. He helped dig a tunnel through a huge mountain named Big Bend. His hammer was 10 feet long and weighed 40 pounds, but he didn't mind. He used it to drive a long steel drill deep into the side of the mountain to clear the way for explosives that blasted away the rock.

The mountain was a mile and a half thick, and the tunnel was deep and dark. Big John Henry worked 12-hour days from sunup to sundown. It was said that John sometimes used two hammers at the same time, one for each arm, which was unheard of in those days. Sometimes, when he swung his hammer down on his drill, the men in the tunnel would run for their lives because they thought the mountain was caving in on them. And Big John would just grin and say, "Sorry, fellas. That's just my hammer you hear sucking in the wind."

2

Now, there were some that thought machines could do a better job on the tunnel than men could, even men like Big John. One day, a salesman wandered into camp with a huge device called a steam drill. He tried to sell it to John's boss, the railroad captain.

When word got to John about this, he rushed over to the captain and cried, "I'll die with a hammer in my hand before I let a machine steal my job from me!"

So the captain made John an offer. John and the other workers could keep their jobs if John raced the steam drill and won. Whoever dug a deeper hole into the side of the mountain within a day would be the winner. Big John didn't hesitate for a moment. He grabbed his hammer and said, "I'll topple this mountain before they can say a machine beat a steel-drivin' man."

4

News of the race spread from town to town, and soon hundreds of people were surrounding the old Big Bend the night before the race. There were people selling food and drink, toy hammers and drills, and even newspapers that read "Big John Battles the Bane of Humanity." No one knew what this meant, but they bought the papers anyway.

John had a good night's rest and ate a hearty meal of two dozen pancakes and a side of ham. By daybreak, he was standing with his hammer in hand by the mouth of the tunnel, ready to teach that machine a lesson.

But the salesman was confident in his steam drill, too. He knew that it would never get tired. It would never slow its pace. It would never need to eat or take a break. And it could drill into rock a whole lot faster than any man could, no matter how big or strong he was. In his opinion, Big John didn't have a chance in the world.

5

But John kept hammering. His pace was steady, and he never missed a stroke. Everyone could see that Big John Henry was true to his word. He would die with a hammer in his hand before he let a machine bring him down.

As the sun set, the whistle blew and the race was finally over. John and the salesman stepped aside as the railroad captain compared the holes they'd made. First, he measured the steam drill's hole. Nine feet! The crowd booed, but the salesman was happy. No man had ever drilled a nine-foot hole into rock in just one day. It was a world record!

Then, the captain went to John's hole. John stood nearby, his hammer still in his hands. The crowd held its breath. The captain placed his measuring tape into the hole and then lifted it out. He turned to the crowd and announced: "Fourteen feet!"

A cheer erupted from the crowd that was so loud, people in Delaware could hear it. Big John Henry had beaten the machine!

7

Soon it was time to begin. The salesman moved the steam drill into position by a wall of rock. John Henry lifted his hammer and stood next to it. The crowd fell silent as the railroad captain lifted his starting gun into the air. On the count of three, he fired a shot. The race had begun!

Some say that when the race started, flames burst from Big John's hammer when it struck a blow. Others claim that the thunderous sound that came from every stroke knocked the people nearby clean off their feet.

The salesman's steam drill was equally impressive. With hardly any effort at all, the machine plowed through the thick rock wall. In just a few minutes, a cloud of dust and debris spread over the sky and blocked out the sun.

As the day passed, the shadows got smaller and then longer again. Big John was standing ankle-deep in a pool of perspiration, and you could see the veins bulging in his massive forearms. You could tell that the hammer was growing heavy in his hands. But the machine next to him showed no signs of slowing down. People were starting to worry about Big John. They wondered how long he could keep this up.

6

Everyone was so happy that no one noticed when John laid his huge hammer on the ground or when he sat down next to it with his back against the mountain. Big John Henry had proven that a person was better than a machine any day, but he would not live to see the end of this one. He died with a big grin on his face and his hammer at his side.

Nowadays, machines make all of our lives easier, but no one will ever forget the day John Henry beat that steam drill. And some days, when the wind is blowing just right, you can still hear his hammer ring.

8

Synonym Search

Match each pair of synonyms in the box below by connecting a word from the first column to a word in the second column. Then, find and circle each synonym pair in the word search. (Hint: Each pair of words is spelled across or down and does not share any letters.)

```
C H O O S E S E L E C T C B Y
Z W X E C R V T B Y N I N Y P
E V Q U I C K F A S T C A Q E
R C R V T B Y N U A S D L V T
R J O Y O U S M E R R Y M E I
O C R V W X Z R V T B Y O S T
R K G E C O M U N Y B T S R E
M C E A W D C R A Y T G T D T
I C N W D E C A Y R O N J I I
S N U W S X Q D E R F V E B N
T V I Q A Z X W S E F G A R Y
A D N Q E T U O L K H F R A V
K D E S X C D F V G B H L C B
E V R A S H A C T H J N Y W N
W C E B E G I N S T A R T E B
A C A W C E R V H U M D E X N
S V L W T B D C W Y O L M F E
C O R R E C T R I G H T A F C
X E C R T U I P L M H F D X V
```

decay   nearly
error   rot
quick   mistake
almost   fast
joyous   start
genuine   select
correct   merry
petite   real
choose   right
begin   tiny

Interpreting a Grid

The children in Mr. Price's class made a **grid** showing the pets they own. Each check mark stands for one pet owned by a child. Use the grid to answer the questions.

Pets Owned by Mr. Price's Students

	Keisha	Juan	Maria	Tim	Anthony
turtle		√			√
rabbit	√	√			
snake	√				
lizard			√	√	
mouse	√	√			
fish		√	√	√	
cat	√	√	√	√	√
dog	√	√	√		√

A. What is the total number of pets listed on the grid? _____

B. Which child owns the most pets? _____

C. Which type of pet is owned by every child? _____

D. How many children own turtles? _____

E. How many more pets does Maria have than Tim? _____

F. Does Anthony have a pet turtle? _____ a rabbit? _____

G. What pets does Juan not own? _____

Finish the Sentences

Read each sentence. Using the word list below, fill in each blank with a word that means the same as the highlighted word in each sentence.

Word List

totally	increase
absent	uncomfortable
detest	strange
talented	remain
error	companion

1. Kim was **missing** from school today because she was _____ .

2. I **hate** ketchup and I _____ mustard, so I ate my hamburger plain.

3. Beside being a **gifted** musician, he is a _____ artist.

4. Mother told us to **stay** in this area, so we'd better _____ here until she returns.

5. I have this **miserable** head cold, and I've felt _____ all day.

6. That's **peculiar**; I've never heard that _____ noise before.

7. I made another **mistake** on my math paper! That's the third _____ I've made today.

8. Jane is a good **friend**, and no one could ask for a better _____ .

9. He hopes that his plants will **multiply** and _____ his earnings.

10. I was **completely** covered with mud, and my clothes were _____ ruined.

Show Your Work

Multiply to solve each problem.

A. 853
    x 25

B. 657
    x 61

C. 574
    x 80

D. 286
    x 51

E. 125
    x 97

F. 913
    x 64

Forming Plurals with y

Complete each sentence with the **plural** form of a noun from the box below.

| bunny | day | family | key | party | penny | strawberry |

1. There are only 10 more _____ until school starts.

2. Grandmother used many _____ to make the pie.

3. Sandra needed a few more _____ to buy the comic book.

4. It takes two _____ to unlock our front door.

5. My pet rabbit gave birth to three baby _____ .

6. I have been to two birthday _____ this week.

7. There were _____ in line at the grocery store.

Forming Plurals with f

Rewrite each word in the box as a **plural** on the line.

1. I would like to buy three _____ of bread.

2. Place the encyclopedias on those _____ .

3. The _____ stood close to their mothers.

4. The _____ were hunting for food.

5. We wore our _____ outside in the snow.

6. A whole is made up of two _____ .

| loaf |
| shelf |
| calf |
| wolf |
| scarf |
| half |

Show Your Work Again

Multiply to solve each problem.

```
 525        917        816
x 51       x 22       x 87
```

```
 950        835        727
x 16       x 10       x 31
```

What's Wrong?

Read each paragraph. Underline the sentence in each paragraph that **does not belong**. The first one has been done for you.

1. Martha's dad is an electrician. He does many different kinds of things when he goes to work. Some days he checks the wiring in peoples' homes. Sometimes he checks the wiring in large buildings and shopping centers. <u>Martha is very proud of him.</u> He often helps put all the electrical wires and outlets in new buildings.

2. Jeremy has many reasons for wanting to be a dentist. He thinks having healthy teeth is very important. He has always been interested in all the things his own dentist does. Jeremy thinks he would be a good dentist, too. He has always enjoyed school.

3. Being a florist takes special training. You must know the names of all the flowers and plants. People who are in the hospital like to receive flowers. You must learn how to care for flowers and plants. It is also important to know how to arrange them.

4. Carl wants to be a teacher, but he can't decide what to teach. At first, he thought he would like to teach math. Then, he thought he would like to teach kindergarten. Carl likes many things. Now he thinks he would like to teach history.

How Much Money?

Calculate the money in each piggy bank and print the total on the line.
Use a dollar sign and a decimal point for each amount.

A.
2 dimes
4 pennies
5 quarters
_____

B.
5 nickels
6 dimes
2 quarters
_____

C.
8 quarters
2 dimes
68 pennies
_____

D.
5 pennies
12 dimes
10 nickels
_____

Contraction Fun

Rewrite the words below as **contractions**. Use the key to create
a patchwork design pattern at the bottom of the page.

1. she will _____

2. you are _____

3. he would _____

4. there is _____

5. I am _____

6. can not _____

7. they are _____

8. should not _____

9. what is _____

10. they will _____

11. we would _____

12. we are _____

If the word ends in	Draw this pattern in the grid
'll	
're	
'd	
's	
'm	
't	

1.	2.	3.	4.
5.	6.	7.	8.
9.	10.	11.	12.

Solve the Code

Multiply and solve the code to find out who wins the race.
Use a calculator.

J	**W**	**N**	**I**
169	512	774	907
x 417	x 692	x 523	x 830

N	**O**	**A**	**S**
825	382	306	614
x 504	x 379	x 168	x 452

70,473	144,778	51,408	404,802	354,304	752,810	415,800	277,528

Prefixes

Choose the correct **prefixes** to form new words below. Write the prefix on the blank in front of each word. Color each box the color listed next to each prefix you choose.

pre – (color red)   **un** – (color blue)   **mis** – (color yellow)   **re** – (color green)

1. _____lead

2. _____tend

3. _____ tell

4. _____ fix

5. _____ fair

6. ____happy

7. _____ flex

8. ___ conduct

9. _____ fill

Analogies

Compare the relationships of the words below.
Find the missing word for each analogy and write it in the space provided.

1. in : out :: up : _____

2. two : four :: three : _____

3. snow : cold :: sun : _____

4. mother : aunt :: father : _____

5. ear : hear :: eye : _____

6. she : her :: he : _____

7. dog : bark :: bird : _____

8. brother : boy :: sister : _____

9. bear : den :: bee : _____

10. finger : hand :: toe : _____

11. girl : mother :: boy : _____

12. left : right :: top : _____

Learning to Divide

Math

Divide to solve each problem.

A. 4⟌32

B. 2⟌10

C. 5⟌45

D. 2⟌18

E. 7⟌35

F. 6⟌54

G. 2⟌12

H. 3⟌36

Division Designs

Divide. Then, connect the dots in order, beginning with the number given first.

Start at 5.

A. 45 ÷ _____ = 5

B. 12 ÷ _____ = 6

C. 36 ÷ _____ = 6

D. 6 ÷ _____ = 2

E. 8 ÷ _____ = 1

F. 35 ÷ _____ = 7

G. 7 ÷ _____ = 1

H. 24 ÷ _____ = 8

I. 42 ÷ _____ = 7

J. 6 ÷ _____ = 3

K. 27 ÷ _____ = 3

L. 2 ÷ _____ = 2

M. 54 ÷ _____ = 9

Start at 6.

A. 18 ÷ _____ = 6

B. 20 ÷ _____ = 5

C. 10 ÷ _____ = 2

D. 24 ÷ _____ = 4

E. 14 ÷ _____ = 7

F. 64 ÷ _____ = 8

G. 5 ÷ _____ = 1

H. 48 ÷ _____ = 6

I. 9 ÷ _____ = 1

J. 42 ÷ _____ = 6

K. 2 ÷ _____ = 1

Linking Verbs

A **linking verb** does not show action but shows a state of being. It connects the subject of a sentence to a word or phrase that describes or renames the subject. Linking verbs include forms of **to be**, such as **am**, **is**, **are**, **was**, and **were**.

Example: The cow **was** black and white.

Read each sentence. Circle the linking verb.

1. Mary was happy when so many people attended her dance recital.
2. Kelsey is sorry she missed the party.
3. Mysteries are my favorite type of book!
4. Today is January third.
5. We were pleased to see our team win the game.
6. Kay was amused when Ken told jokes.
7. I am anxious to finish my homework before dinner.
8. Mr. Alton was quiet during the concert.

Identifying Parts of Speech

Read each sentence. Decide if the highlighted word is an **adjective,** an **adverb,** a **noun,** or a **verb**. Use the key to write **Adj**, **Adv**, **N**, or **V**, on the line.

	Key		
Adj – adjective	**Adv – adverb**	**N – noun**	**V – verb**

_____ 1. The **big**, red apple fell off the tree.

_____ 2. The yellow **dog** followed Trina.

_____ 3. Sarah **fell** down the stairs.

_____ 4. **Broccoli** is on sale at the market today.

_____ 5. Kenny **slowly** walked to school.

_____ 6. My **new** sweater is very warm.

_____ 7. Mariah **sprinted** across the meadow.

_____ 8. The **winner** of the race cried tears of joy.

_____ 9. The **tornado** did not damage any homes.

Story Problems

Solve the story problems.

A. Patricia bought 16 doughnuts for herself and her 3 friends. If they each eat the same number of doughnuts, how many will each person eat?

_____

B. Catherine has 7 days to knit 21 sweaters. If she knits the same number of sweaters each day, how many will she have to make each day?

_____

C. Victoria picked 72 apples and used them to make pies. She used 6 apples in each pie. How many pies did Victoria make?

_____

Descriptive Writing

Read the short paragraph.

It was a nice day. Without warning, a storm suddenly
flew in over the lake. We were afraid our boat would sink.

Here are some adjectives that can help describe the sentences:

What kind of day it was: bright, sunny, lovely, warm, spring

How the storm came in: quickly, gusting, swirling, howling, thundering, booming

What the storm looked like: dark, cloudy, windy, blackness, inky

What the people looked like: pale, tense, worried, frightened

Rewrite the paragraph to make it more colorful and interesting.
Use the adjectives above or think of your own to describe what has
happened in the paragraph. Give the paragraph a title.

_____

_____

_____

_____

_____

_____

_____

_____

_____

Beat the Clock (Division Facts 0 to 9)

A.	36 ÷ 6 =	8 ÷ 1 =	45 ÷ 9 =	16 ÷ 8 =	35 ÷ 5 =
B.	24 ÷ 8 =	27 ÷ 9 =	20 ÷ 5 =	21 ÷ 3 =	8 ÷ 2 =
C.	20 ÷ 4 =	42 ÷ 7 =	18 ÷ 6 =	14 ÷ 2 =	28 ÷ 7 =
D.	56 ÷ 8 =	9 ÷ 3 =	3 ÷ 1 =	40 ÷ 8 =	12 ÷ 4 =
E.	10 ÷ 2 =	48 ÷ 6 =	45 ÷ 5 =	0 ÷ 6 =	15 ÷ 3 =
F.	7 ÷ 7 =	6 ÷ 2 =	18 ÷ 9 =	7 ÷ 1 =	32 ÷ 4 =
G.	5 ÷ 1 =	35 ÷ 5 =	56 ÷ 7 =	5 ÷ 5 =	30 ÷ 3 =
H.	18 ÷ 6 =	15 ÷ 5 =	18 ÷ 2 =	72 ÷ 8 =	2 ÷ 1 =
I.	30 ÷ 5 =	1 ÷ 1 =	21 ÷ 7 =	8 ÷ 4 =	0 ÷ 3 =
J.	9 ÷ 9 =	28 ÷ 4 =	16 ÷ 4 =	12 ÷ 2 =	36 ÷ 9 =
K.	8 ÷ 8 =	27 ÷ 3 =	6 ÷ 6 =	6 ÷ 3 =	0 ÷ 4 =
L.	12 ÷ 3 =	81 ÷ 9 =	0 ÷ 2 =	49 ÷ 7 =	36 ÷ 9 =
M.	30 ÷ 6 =	32 ÷ 8 =	9 ÷ 1 =	0 ÷ 8 =	14 ÷ 7 =
N.	35 ÷ 7 =	16 ÷ 2 =	0 ÷ 7 =	42 ÷ 6 =	6 ÷ 1 =
O.	45 ÷ 9 =	24 ÷ 4 =	10 ÷ 5 =	0 ÷ 1 =	12 ÷ 6 =
P.	2 ÷ 2 =	0 ÷ 5 =	24 ÷ 6 =	40 ÷ 5 =	24 ÷ 3 =
Q.	54 ÷ 6 =	27 ÷ 9 =	18 ÷ 3 =	25 ÷ 5 =	63 ÷ 9 =
R.	64 ÷ 8 =	4 ÷ 1 =	4 ÷ 4 =	0 ÷ 9 =	4 ÷ 2 =
S.	72 ÷ 8 =	63 ÷ 7 =	48 ÷ 8 =	27 ÷ 9 =	24 ÷ 8 =
T.	36 ÷ 4 =	54 ÷ 9 =	3 ÷ 3 =	40 ÷ 5 =	14 ÷ 7 =

Time:

Number correct:

Sentences & Fragments

Read each group of words. If the group is only a fragment, write **F** on the line. If it is a sentence, write **S** on the line and add the correct ending punctuation. The first one has been done for you.

___S___ **1.** Isabelle is a good dancer .

_____ **2.** To the park

_____ **3.** Ride in the car

_____ **4.** Be careful

_____ **5.** Stacey liked the movie

_____ **6.** Will you come over tomorrow

_____ **7.** On top of the house by the chimney

Division Designs

Fill in the missing **divisors**. Then, connect the dots in order, beginning with the number given first.

Start at 6.

A. 30 ÷ _____ = 6	**F.** 56 ÷ _____ = 8
B. 15 ÷ _____ = 5	**G.** 6 ÷ _____ = 1
C. 28 ÷ _____ = 4	**H.** 21 ÷ _____ = 7
D. 20 ÷ _____ = 4	**I.** 40 ÷ _____ = 5
E. 9 ÷ _____ = 9	**J.** 48 ÷ _____ = 8

Start at 2.

A. 5 ÷ _____ = 5	**G.** 45 ÷ _____ = 9
B. 63 ÷ _____ = 9	**H.** 12 ÷ _____ = 4
C. 9 ÷ _____ = 3	**I.** 21 ÷ _____ = 3
D. 8 ÷ _____ = 4	**J.** 63 ÷ _____ = 7
E. 18 ÷ _____ = 3	**K.** 25 ÷ _____ = 5
F. 56 ÷ _____ = 7	

Complete Subjects

Draw a line under the **complete subject** of each sentence below.

1. Astronauts are very brave people.
2. Donna's birthday is today.
3. The big, red boat sped across the water.
4. The spectators enjoyed the fireworks.
5. Barbara and Cindy love to garden.
6. The blue engine stopped at the station.
7. The actor was excellent in the play.
8. The movie was the best one I have ever seen!
9. Good health is important to everyone.
10. All children love to play.
11. The pictures in that book are beautiful.
12. The raft floated across the lake.

>, =, or <

Math

Divide to solve each problem. Write **>**, **=**, or **<** to compare the answers.

A. $5\overline{)25}$ B. $7\overline{)35}$

C. $3\overline{)27}$ D. $4\overline{)32}$

E. $8\overline{)56}$ F. $7\overline{)49}$

G. $2\overline{)18}$ H. $9\overline{)36}$

A $\square$ F

D $\square$ B

C $\square$ G

E $\square$ H

Division Practice

Divide to solve each problem.

A. $4\overline{)24}$ B. $9\overline{)72}$ C. $4\overline{)36}$ D. $7\overline{)70}$

E. $2\overline{)12}$ F. $4\overline{)16}$

G. $2\overline{)20}$ H. $3\overline{)21}$

Conjunctions

Select the correct **conjunction** to complete each sentence. Write it on the line.

and	but	or

1. I have enough money to buy both a ball _____ a bat.

2. You may have either milk _____ juice to drink.

3. Her favorite sandwich is peanut butter _____ jelly.

4. John took swimming lessons, _____ he still could not swim.

5. Mom said I can choose either pancakes _____ waffles.

6. We will go either to the mountains _____ the ocean on our vacation.

7. The United States' flag is red, white, _____ blue.

8. Johnny worked very hard on his report, _____ he only made a B.

Understanding What I've Read

Independence Day

The Fourth of July is an important holiday for the United States. It is Independence Day. On July 4, 1776, the United States declared, or stated, that it was a country. It would no longer be part of England. "Independence" means to take care of yourself without help from others. That is why July 4 is called Independence Day. Every Fourth of July people in the United States celebrate the beginning of the country. There are parades, speeches, and lots of fireworks. People fly their flags to show they are proud of their country.

1. What is the main idea of this story?
   a. The founding of the United States is celebrated on July 4.
   b. Parades are common on July 4.
   c. July 4 is for fireworks.

2. On what day does the United States celebrate its independence?

   _____

3. What word means **to state or say**?
   a. declare
   b. celebrate
   c. fireworks

4. What are some ways people celebrate Independence Day?

   _____

   _____

5. From whom did the United States declare its independence?

   _____

6. What does the word **independent** mean?
   a. holiday
   b. stated
   c. free and on your own

Division

Divide to solve each problem.

A. 56 ÷ 7 = _____   B. 24 ÷ 8 = _____   C. 54 ÷ 9 = _____

D. 32 ÷ 8 = _____   E. 12 ÷ 3 = _____   F. 25 ÷ 5 = _____

G. 50 ÷ 5 = _____   H. 42 ÷ 7 = _____   I. 72 ÷ 9 = _____

J. 66 ÷ 6 = _____   K. 40 ÷ 5 = _____   L. 21 ÷ 3 = _____

Main Idea

Reading Comprehension

The **main idea** of a paragraph is its central thought or topic. Read each paragraph and the three phrases below it. Decide which one tells the main idea. Write the letter of that phrase on the line.

_____   1.   Taffy's little brother was missing again. At least, no one knew where he was. Little Jeff could get into the strangest places. He would stay hidden until everyone got worried or mad. His favorite place to hide was in the clothes hamper. Taffy's mother said they should put a bell on Jeff!

a. A mischievous boy   **b.** The clothes hamper   **c.** Taffy's family

_____   2.   Waterskiing is a lot of fun once you learn how. Sailing and boating are nice ways to spend a summer day. Water polo is fun to play. If you are near the ocean, bodysurfing and windsurfing are really exciting.

a. Summertime   **b.** Water sports   **c.** Waterskiing

_____   3.   Ted asked his dad if he could have an allowance. Ted's dad said that he certainly could! He also said that Ted would have to do a few chores around the house. That was how he would earn his allowance. Every week Ted had to mow the lawn. He also had to take out the garbage. Ted had only been earning an allowance for three weeks. He was already thinking of asking for a raise!

a. Cleaning the garage   **b.** Ted and his dad   **c.** Earning an allowance

Writing Sentences

Read each pair of sentences. Rewrite the facts in a single sentence on the line.

1. Anna went to the beach. Anna wore her new bathing suit.
   _____

2. Billy hit a home run. Billy's team voted him the player of the game.
   _____

3. Charlie fell down the steps. Charlie was embarrassed.
   _____

4. Dianne went to the mall. Dianne bought a pair of jeans.
   _____

5. Eric painted a picture. Eric got paint on the floor.
   _____

6. Fran went to Gina's house. Fran and Gina played games.
   _____

Division Facts

Divide to solve each problem.

A. 63 ÷ 9 = _____   B. 49 ÷ 7 = _____   C. 15 ÷ 3 = _____

D. 64 ÷ 8 = _____   E. 30 ÷ 6 = _____   F. 80 ÷ 8 = _____

G. 12 ÷ 2 = _____   H. 45 ÷ 5 = _____   I. 81 ÷ 9 = _____

Magic Trail

Follow the trail by solving the math problems. Can you find the magic number?

4 x 3 = ☐   − 8 = ☐

÷ 4 = ☐

+ 11 = ☐

x 4 = ☐

÷ 8 = ☐

x 1 = ☐

÷ 6 = ☐   + 7 = ☐   − 3 = ☐

÷ 5 = ☐

x 7 = ☐

x 12 = ☐

− 2 = ☐

÷ 3 = ☐

+ 6 = ☐

x 5 = ☐

Magic Number ◯

− 6 = ☐   + 4 = ☐

x 1 = ☐   − 6 = ☐   x 2 = ☐   + 3 = ☐

Constructing Stories

Create a short story by answering the questions about the picture.
Use adjectives for description.

1. Who or what is this story about?

   _____

2. Where does this story take place?

   _____

3. How does this story begin?

   _____

4. What will happen next? _____

   _____

5. How will the story end? _____

   _____

Write a short story using the information above. Be sure to use capital letters and periods.
Remember to indent the first sentence and give your story a title.

_____

_____

_____

_____

_____

Division with Remainders

Divide to solve each problem.

A. $7\overline{)52}$ B. $9\overline{)83}$ C. $6\overline{)40}$ D. $5\overline{)29}$

E. $9\overline{)42}$ F. $3\overline{)55}$ G. $5\overline{)27}$ H. $2\overline{)37}$

Using Suffixes

Look at each word below. Write the **suffix** from the box that makes sense with the word on the line. Note that some words may have more than one possible answer.

er	ful	less	ly	ness

1. paint_____
2. mouth_____
3. sorrow_____
4. bowl_____
5. teach_____
6. shy_____
7. event_____
8. harm_____
9. quick_____
10. care_____
11. will_____
12. motion_____
13. coward_____
14. cheer_____
15. loud_____
16. nice_____
17. help_____
18. price_____

Word Box Stories

Write eight words about the picture in the word box. Use the words to write a story.
Be sure to use adjectives, capital letters, and periods. Give your story a title.

Things to Think About

Who is this story about?   Where does this story take place?

How does this story begin?   What happens next?

How will this story end?

Word Box

_____ _____

_____ _____

_____ _____

_____ _____

_____

_____

_____

_____

_____

_____

_____

_____

Root Words

Look at each word below. Write each **root word** on the line.

1. nonsense

2. rewrite

3. spoonful

4. happiness

_____

5. kindness

6. brotherhood

7. ticklish

8. quickly

_____

9. baker

10. lovable

11. helpless

12. cleanness

_____

Three-Digit Dividends

Divide to solve each problem.

A. $5\overline{)125}$

B. $6\overline{)468}$

C. $4\overline{)632}$

D. $9\overline{)945}$

E. $8\overline{)704}$

F. $2\overline{)778}$

G. $7\overline{)672}$

H. $7\overline{)784}$

Predicates

The **simple predicate** is a verb that tells what the subject did or what was done to the subject. The **complete predicate** includes the verb and all of the words that tell more about it.

Example: The white cat slept on the pillow.

The simple predicate is **slept** and the complete predicate is **slept on the pillow**.

Underline the complete predicate of each sentence. Circle the simple predicate.

1. Bess danced in the school play.
2. We went to the mall after the library.
3. California is a state on the West Coast.
4. The weather began to turn cool.
5. It rained for hours yesterday!
6. Opal made a painting for her mom.
7. Snow fell for six hours.
8. Seven students were in the spelling bee.
9. The tractor made a loud noise.
10. We served ice cream and cake at the party.

Word Problems with Division

Read the word problems below. Solve each problem.

A.   Jim, Steve, and Earl chartered a fishing boat. The trip cost $36. The men divided the cost of the trip between them equally. How much did each man have to pay?

$ _____

B.   Jen has 21 dolls. If she puts the same number of dolls in 3 different doll houses, how many dolls will she put in each house?

_____ dolls

C.   Mabel had a dinner party for her friends. She prepared 24 meals and set up 4 tables. She wanted the same number of people at each table. How many people did she put at each table?

_____ people

113

Main Idea

Circle or write the **main idea** of each paragraph.

1.   It is September. It is the night of the first football game of the year. Everyone at Kidwell School is excited. Most excited of all is Cliff. This is the very first night he has ever marched with the band. He holds his clarinet nervously. As the director's white glove raises up, Cliff's heart skips a beat. He has dreamed of this moment and it is finally here. He is a member of the marching band.

    a. Cliff's first football game as a band member
    b. Excitement on the night of the first game
    c. Cliff and his friends at the football game

2.   There are many different eyeglass frames. Some are very large. Some are simple and some are fancy. Carol liked every pair she chose. Her favorite pair looked like blue ovals.

The main idea is: _____

Money Word Problems

Solve each word problem.

A.   Joe and Sam earned $24 raking leaves. They divided the money evenly between them. How much did each person get?

$ _____

B.   Mrs. Smith made 12 tacos. She gave her 4 children an equal number of tacos. How many tacos did each child receive?

_____ tacos

C.   Jamie and Eddie bought a pack of art paper. The pack contained 20 pieces of paper. If they each take the same amount of paper, how many pieces will they each get?

_____ pieces

D.   Randi has a package of candy containing 49 pieces. If she wanted to eat an equal share of the candy every day for 7 days, how many pieces would she eat each day?

_____ pieces

The American Heroine

1

Deborah was born in Plympton, Massachusetts, in 1760. Her family was very poor. They sent her to live as a servant with the Thomas family where she took care of their 10 sons. She worked hard on the Thomas farm. When she did her chores, she wore men's clothing since it was easier than wearing a long dress. Deborah was not sent to school, so she taught herself to read and write at night.

By the age of 18, Deborah had grown to be five feet eight inches tall, which was very tall for that time period. She was very strong, too, from years of farm work. But Deborah decided to give up life on the farm. Instead, she became a schoolteacher and taught students in a one-room schoolhouse. At night, she listened to stories men told of the war against England.

3

Many brave soldiers fought in the American Revolutionary War. Frank Shurtliff was one of them. He was severely wounded in battle, yet he returned to keep fighting. His fellow soldiers admired him. Little did they know, Frank was really a woman in disguise.

Have you ever been told that you couldn't do something, but you went ahead and did it anyway? That is exactly what Deborah Samson did back in 1782. She changed her identity to a man. Then, she joined the American Army to fight against the British.

In those days, women were not allowed to become soldiers. The only way for Deborah to fight for her country was to pretend to be a man. It was a dangerous thing to do, but she felt it was her patriotic duty to face the British on the front lines.

2

For a long time, the American colonists had been upset with the way the British were treating them. They felt they were unfairly taxed and didn't have the right to vote on what happened in their own towns and cities. They couldn't speak freely and British soldiers often stayed in their homes uninvited.

Then, the Americans signed the Declaration of Independence and the country went to war with England. Many of the men Deborah knew were joining the army to fight. Deborah was angry with what the British were doing, too. She also wanted to help free her country. It wasn't fair that they wouldn't let her become a soldier just because she was a woman. Deborah decided to do her duty anyway.

4

Deborah disguised herself as a man by cutting her hair and wearing men's clothes. At first, she signed the papers to join and then changed her mind. But after a little while, she gathered up her courage and tried again. This time, it worked. She signed her name as Frank Shurtliff and no one suspected that she was really a woman. Her disguise worked. Deborah Samson had become a soldier.

Just three days later, Deborah, now known as Frank, had a uniform and orders to march.

5

Deborah Samson was awarded an Honorable Discharge from the military. She returned home to her family in Massachusetts. Soon after, the Americans won the war.

Two years later, Deborah married a farmer named Benjamin Gannett. They had three children but were very poor. Her friend Paul Revere, the famous messenger of the war, helped her receive the money she was owed for fighting in the army. Then, once Deborah's story started to spread, people paid to hear her tell stories about her adventures. Everyone knew her as "the American Heroine."

7

By 1782, the war was almost over, but there was still a lot of fighting going on in the state of New York. Most of the combat was very dangerous. Deborah fought bravely in several of these battles. The other soldiers saw that she was a very strong and courageous warrior. They were honored to serve with her in battle.

Then, Deborah was wounded when her unit was ambushed by enemy troops. She received injuries to the head and leg. She was afraid that the doctor would discover that she was really a woman, so she limped away from the hospital when the doctor wasn't looking. Then, she treated her wounds herself.

Shortly afterwards, Deborah returned to battle. She continued to fight until she collapsed one day with a brain fever. This time, the doctor who found her was surprised to find that Frank Shurtliff was really a woman in disguise.

In 1983, 200 years after she fought to defend her country, Deborah Samson was named the "Official Heroine of the Commonwealth of Massachusetts." This was the first time an award like this was given to anyone in the United States. A statue was also erected for Deborah in her hometown.

Because of women like Deborah Samson and their willingness to take chances for what they believed, women now serve as soldiers and are a proud part of the United States Armed Forces. Deborah's heroics and bravery will not be forgotten.

Identifying Misspelled Words

Underline the spelling error in each sentence.
Write the correct spelling on the line.

1. Missy tripped while she was runing. _____

2. Do you beleeve that story? _____

3. Valentine's Day is in Febuary. _____

4. I take gymnastics classes on Wensdays. _____

5. Mother made apple pie for desert. _____

6. I like to walk to scool. _____

7. Sara is going to the beech on Saturday. _____

8. It is cool outside, so I will wear a sweter. _____

Adding Fractions

Math

Add the fractions.

A. $\dfrac{5}{8}$
$+\dfrac{2}{8}$

B. $\dfrac{4}{9}$
$+\dfrac{3}{9}$

C. $\dfrac{9}{12}$
$+\dfrac{1}{12}$

D. $\dfrac{1}{6}$
$+\dfrac{4}{6}$

E. $\dfrac{2}{5}$
$+\dfrac{3}{5}$

F. $\dfrac{2}{4}$
$+\dfrac{1}{4}$

G. $\dfrac{3}{5}$
$+\dfrac{1}{5}$

H. $\dfrac{1}{6}$
$+\dfrac{4}{6}$

Words into Math

Use the table to answer the questions.
If the information needed to answer a question is not given, write **NG**.

Daily Schedule	Time
Homeroom	8:00 – 8:10
1st Period	8:15 – 9:15
2nd Period	9:20 – 10:25
3rd Period	10:25 – 11:25
Lunch	11:25 – 12:00
4th Period	12:00 – 1:15
5th Period	1:05 – 2:05
6th Period	2:10 – 3:10

Charles High School has this daily schedule. It names all of the class periods and gives the time each one starts and ends.

1. How long is each class period?

_____

2. If Jimmy gets to class at 8:30, how much of 1st period has he missed?

_____

3. What class does Susan have 4th period?

_____

4. Kaitlin's mom picked her up at 2:00. During what period did she leave?

_____

5. Jamal stays in Mr. Wood's room for 2nd and 3rd periods. How long is he in that room?

_____

6. During what period does Ms. Smith teach gym?

_____

7. How long is the lunch period?

_____

8. Which period begins at 9:20?

_____

9. What event happens between 8:00 and 8:10 each morning?

_____

10. If school is over after 6th period, what time do the students get out?

_____

Story Web

Finish the story web. Use the words in the web to write a story.
Be sure to use capital letters and periods. Give your story a title.

THINGS TO THINK ABOUT

Who is this story about?   Where does this story take place?

How does this story begin?   What happens next?

How will this story end?

feet   spaceship

trolley   transportation   bicycle

_____

_____

Division Facts 9–12 Review

Divide to solve each problem.

A. 9)90 B. 10)20 C. 11)99 D. 12)108 E. 11)77

F. 12)24 G. 10)60 H. 12)60 I. 11)110 J. 10)100

K. 9)27 L. 9)9 M. 10)120 N. 11)121 O. 9)108

Topic Sentence

A **topic sentence** is a sentence in a paragraph that tells the main idea.

Example: **Ellen disliked all types of tiny, crawling things.** Spiders made her crazy. Worms gave her the willies. Little, shiny lizards made Ellen feel awful. The only tiny, crawling thing Ellen liked was her little brother Ned.

Read each paragraph. Underline the topic sentence.

1. Raccoons sleep all day. They wake up at night to get food when they are hungry. Fireflies blink on and off at night. Owls hunt for their food after the sun goes down. Bats search for insects after dark. These are all night creatures.

2. There are many interesting things at the hairstyling shop. There is the stylist's chair that spins around and goes up and down. There are all the different combs, lotions, and special things the stylist uses. Some people like the magazines in the waiting area. Some folks like the hairstyles they get the best!

3. The takeoff was surprisingly smooth. The sky was clear and there were only a few clouds. The flight attendants were all very friendly. Amanda thought her dinner on the plane was delicious. In fact, everything about Amanda's first airplane ride was perfect.

Math Puzzle

Solve the problems below and write the answers in the boxes.
On the building, shade in the squares that match your answers.
The answers will make a pattern.

5 x 3 – 6 = ☐

27 ÷ 3 + 4 = ☐

3 x 6 ÷ 9 = ☐

120 ÷ 10 x 11 = ☐

32 ÷ 8 + 7 = ☐

4 x 3 – 9 = ☐

2 x 3 x 5 = ☐

21 ÷ 7 + 4 = ☐

81 ÷ 9 + 8 = ☐

3 x 2 + 8 = ☐

40 ÷ 5 + 8 = ☐

56 ÷ 7 + 7 = ☐

5 x 8 ÷ 10 = ☐

4 x 9 ÷ 3 = ☐

2 x 9 ÷ 3 = ☐

33 ÷ 3 – 6 = ☐

16	3	30	14
8	34	45	27
25	18	19	51
5	40	23	12
17	70	92	6
132	10	67	9
11	53	32	2
20	22	83	36
20	60	33	78
13	4	15	7

Constructing Stories

Things to Think About for Every Story

- Every sentence begins with a capital letter and ends with a period, question mark, or exclamation mark.
- A paragraph contains a main idea and supporting details.
- The first line of a paragraph should be indented.
- Adjectives make stories more colorful and interesting.
- A story tells who did what, when, where, how, and why.
- Stories have a beginning, a middle, and an end.

Write a story about performing on stage. Be sure to follow all of the tips provided. Remember to indent the first sentence of each paragraph and give your story a title.

_____

Solve the Code

You must solve the code to find the alligator's name and cross the stream.
For each answer in the code, write the letter of the corresponding problem.

N
4$\overline{)933}$

E
8$\overline{)930}$

N
5$\overline{)732}$

I
3$\overline{)913}$

D
9$\overline{)994}$

M
6$\overline{)980}$

A
5$\overline{)844}$

S
2$\overline{)827}$

H
9$\overline{)933}$

W
7$\overline{)802}$

S
7$\overline{)934}$

I
3$\overline{)503}$

E
6$\overline{)759}$

R
8$\overline{)981}$

A
4$\overline{)694}$

$\overline{\text{103 R6}}$ $\overline{\text{304 R1}}$ $\overline{\text{133 R3}}$ $\overline{\text{233 R1}}$ $\overline{\text{173 R2}}$ $\overline{\text{163 R2}}$ $\overline{\text{126 R3}}$

$\overline{\text{167 R2}}$ $\overline{\text{413 R1}}$

$\overline{\text{168 R4}}$ $\overline{\text{146 R2}}$ $\overline{\text{110 R4}}$ $\overline{\text{122 R5}}$ $\overline{\text{116 R2}}$ $\overline{\text{114 R4}}$.

Topic Sentence

A **topic sentence** is a sentence in a paragraph that tells the main idea.
Underline the topic sentence in each paragraph.

1. Learning to play the piano was not always easy for Todd. He did not always feel like practicing. Sometimes he made a lot of mistakes, even when he was trying hard. Some days, Todd would feel too tired to play. When Todd did start to get better, though, he was very proud.

2. Kim and Kurt spent $10 each for their stamp albums. Kim bought four special stamps from France. They cost $1 each. Kurt spent $6 on a set of Olympic stamps. Collecting stamps was going to be expensive for the children!

3. Winters can be very hard in Vermont. There are often heavy snowfalls with high winds. It can be days before some back roads are plowed. Many people in Vermont chop their own wood. That's very hard work. Many people drive special cars and trucks to get around on the snowy roads.

Adding Fractions

Add. Write each answer in simplest form. The first one has been done for you.

A. $\dfrac{2}{5} + \dfrac{1}{5} = \boxed{\dfrac{3}{5}}$

B. $\dfrac{3}{5} + \dfrac{1}{5} = \boxed{}$

C. $\dfrac{7}{9} + \dfrac{1}{9} = \boxed{}$

D. $\dfrac{1}{5} + \dfrac{2}{5} = \boxed{}$

E. $\dfrac{3}{8} + \dfrac{4}{8} = \boxed{}$

F. $\dfrac{5}{7} + \dfrac{1}{7} = \boxed{}$

F. $\dfrac{1}{4} + \dfrac{3}{4} = \boxed{}$

G. $\dfrac{5}{6} + \dfrac{2}{6} = \boxed{}$

Fraction Addition

Add. Write each answer in simplest form. The first one has been done for you.

A. $\dfrac{1}{6} + \dfrac{1}{6} = \boxed{\dfrac{1}{3}}$

B. $\dfrac{3}{10} + \dfrac{1}{10} = \boxed{}$

C. $\dfrac{1}{7} + \dfrac{3}{7} = \boxed{}$

D. $\dfrac{6}{7} + \dfrac{3}{7} = \boxed{}$

E. $\dfrac{1}{8} + \dfrac{3}{8} = \boxed{}$

F. $\dfrac{2}{9} + \dfrac{5}{9} = \boxed{}$

G. $\dfrac{5}{9} + \dfrac{1}{9} = \boxed{}$

H. $\dfrac{2}{5} + \dfrac{3}{5} = \boxed{}$

Adjectives

Find and underline the **adjectives** in each paragraph.

1.   Anna went to the big shoe store with her mother. Anna needed some new shoes. She saw black, shiny shoes and white, ruffled shoes. Anna especially liked the fancy red dress shoes with black and white trim. Anna decided to buy some tan shoes. Anna's mother paid the tall salesman, and Anna wore her new shoes home.

2.   I like to watch the brave firefighters work. They wear large, protective outfits to keep them safe from fire. Firefighters try to save small houses, big houses, and office buildings. They will put out a fire anywhere. Sometimes, I have watched them put out fires in the tall forest behind my neighborhood. I would like to be a brave firefighter when I grow up.

Writing in the Third Person

This story is written from the first person **point of view**. Rewrite the story below, changing the point of view to third person. Add an ending to the story.

A Skating Disaster

I was skating on the sidewalk a few blocks from my house yesterday afternoon when a dog darted out of the bushes. The dog ran right across my path. Boom! Down I fell! I stood up and brushed myself off. Suddenly, a little boy ran out of the same bushes. The boy was calling, "Come back, Pixie!" As he rushed past me, I fell down again. I had just picked myself up again when a man raced out of the bushes! He was shouting, "Come back, Sergio! Come back, Pixie!" I . . .

_____

_____

_____

_____

_____

_____

_____

_____

_____

_____

_____

_____

Analogies

Compare the relationships of the words below.
Write a word on the line to complete each analogy.

1. car : driver : : plane : _____

2. bird : sky : : fish : _____

3. coffee : drink : : hamburger : _____

4. small : tiny : : large : _____

5. glove : hand : : boot : _____

6. easy : simple : : hard : _____

7. breakfast : lunch : : morning : _____

8. blue : color : : round : _____

9. date : calendar : : time : _____

10. win : lose : : stop : _____

Subtracting Fractions

Math

Subtract. Write each answer in simplest form. The first one has been done for you.

A.
$$\frac{2}{3} - \frac{1}{3} = \boxed{\frac{1}{3}}$$

B.
$$\frac{7}{9} - \frac{5}{9} = \boxed{}$$

C.
$$\frac{3}{7} - \frac{1}{7} = \boxed{}$$

D.
$$\frac{3}{5} - \frac{1}{5} = \boxed{}$$

E.
$$\frac{5}{8} - \frac{2}{8} = \boxed{}$$

F.
$$\frac{3}{4} - \frac{1}{4} = \boxed{}$$

G.
$$\frac{8}{9} - \frac{3}{9} = \boxed{}$$

H.
$$\frac{4}{6} - \frac{2}{6} = \boxed{}$$

Mixed Problem Puzzle

Solve the problems. Use the number key at the bottom of the page to color the picture.

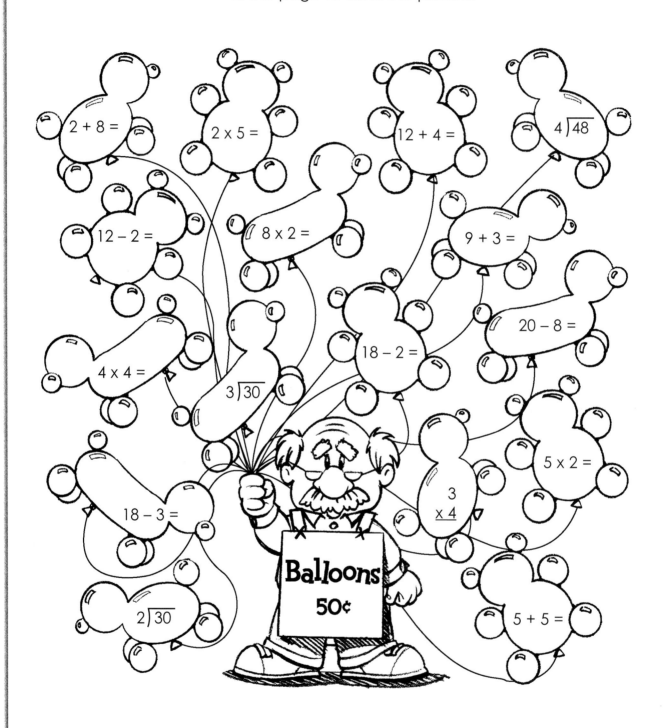

2 + 8 =

2 x 5 =

12 + 4 =

4⟌48

12 − 2 =

8 x 2 =

9 + 3 =

4 x 4 =

3⟌30

18 − 2 =

20 − 8 =

18 − 3 =

3
x 4

5 x 2 =

2⟌30

Balloons
50¢

5 + 5 =

10 = yellow   16 = orange
15 = green   12 = purple

Completing Analogies

Fill in the blanks to complete the **analogies**.

1. **Ice** is to **cold** as **steam** is to _____.

2. The **sun** is to **daytime** as the **moon** is to _____.

3. **Perspiration** is to **heat** as **shivering** is to _____.

4. **Birds** are to **flying** as **dolphins** are to _____.

5. **Books** are to **reading** as **radios** are to _____.

6. **Shoes** are to **feet** as **gloves** are to _____.

Subtracting Fractions

Subtract the fractions. Write each answer in simplest form.

A. $\dfrac{6}{7} - \dfrac{2}{7}$

B. $\dfrac{6}{9} - \dfrac{3}{9}$

C. $\dfrac{9}{10} - \dfrac{5}{10}$

D. $\dfrac{5}{8} - \dfrac{2}{8}$

E. $\dfrac{3}{4} - \dfrac{1}{4}$

F. $\dfrac{2}{5} - \dfrac{1}{5}$

G. $\dfrac{8}{9} - \dfrac{1}{9}$

H. $\dfrac{2}{3} - \dfrac{1}{3}$

Writing in the First Person

This story is written from the third person **point of view**. Rewrite the story, changing the point of view to first person. Add an ending to the story.

Soccer Hero

Joey has been playing soccer for three years. His team is called the Mountain Lions. Joey plays goalie on the team. A goalie tries to keep the other team from scoring by standing in front of the net and blocking any balls kicked toward it. Joey is a great goalie. He played on the All-Star Team last year. Last Thursday, the Mountain Lions played a team called the Blazing Suns. The Suns were ahead by two goals. The game was almost over and it looked like the Lions were going to lose. Joey . . .

_____

_____

_____

_____

_____

_____

_____

_____

_____

_____

_____

_____

Proofreading

Circle each letter that should be capitalized.
Add punctuation marks in the proper places.
Write an ending to the story.

Creature from Outer Space

tim and i decided to camp out in the backyard we
got our sleeping bags two flashlights and some snacks
we unrolled our sleeping bags lay down and began to
munch on some pretzels it was a clear night and the
stars were sparkling brightly tim found the big dipper
and the north star one bright star seemed to be moving
we watched it race across the sky suddenly it stopped
and began to grow bigger it was coming toward us it
came to a stop right over our heads now we could see
that it was not a star at all it was a spaceship a beam of
light shot from the spaceship and glowed all around
tim . . .

_____

_____

_____

_____

_____

_____

_____

Tic-Tac-Toe Synonyms

In each tic-tac-toe grid, circle three words in a row that are **synonyms**.

1.

big	above	over
love	large	below
old	hate	giant

2.

front	awful	baby
back	terrible	good
start	horrible	lovely

3.

cry	whisper	sing
weep	spell	come
sob	silly	rise

4.

wet	hot	cold
near	icy	warm
chilly	rain	far

Math # Adding & Subtracting Fractions

Add or **subtract** the mixed numbers. Write each answer in simplest form.

A. $3\dfrac{3}{5}$
$+\ 5\dfrac{1}{5}$

B. $2\dfrac{2}{3}$
$-\ 1\dfrac{1}{3}$

C. $8\dfrac{9}{11}$
$-\ 4\dfrac{5}{11}$

D. $6\dfrac{3}{4}$
$-\ 2\dfrac{1}{4}$

E. $4\dfrac{4}{8}$
$+\ 3\dfrac{2}{8}$

F. $9\dfrac{2}{6}$
$+\ 1\dfrac{2}{6}$

Mixed Problems <, >, or =

Read each problem. Write the correct symbol (<, >, or =) on the line.

A. 60.5 _____ 60

B. 6 x 4 _____ 8 x 3

C. 3,345 _____ 4,002

D. 95 _____ 93

E. 72.5 _____ 72.1

F. 40 x 2 _____ 3 x 30

G. 145,092 _____ 147,958

H. $\frac{8}{9}$ _____ $\frac{7}{9}$

I. 50.3 _____ 50.2

J. 97.05 _____ 97.50

K. $\frac{12}{12}$ _____ $\frac{8}{8}$

Words into Math

Read the story and answer the questions below.
If the information needed to answer a question is not given, write **NG**.

Mrs. Grom's fourth grade class is going on a field trip to the zoo. There are 25 students in her class. Each child must pay $2.00 to get into the zoo and $1.27 for bus fare. The class left the school at 9:00 A.M. and returned at 2:20 P.M.

1. What was the total each student paid to go on this trip?

   _____

2. How much money did Mrs. Grom collect from the class altogether?

   _____

3. One parent for every 5 students came along on the trip. How many parents came?

   _____

4. Did Daniel like the sharks or the polar bears better?

   _____

5. How long was the class gone from school?

   _____

6. How much did the zoo collect for all 25 students?

   _____

7. How much more did it cost each child to get into the zoo than to ride the bus?

   _____

8. Did the students behave nicely on this trip?

   _____

Antonym Puzzle

Color the areas green that contain pairs of **antonyms**.
Color the rest of the design yellow.

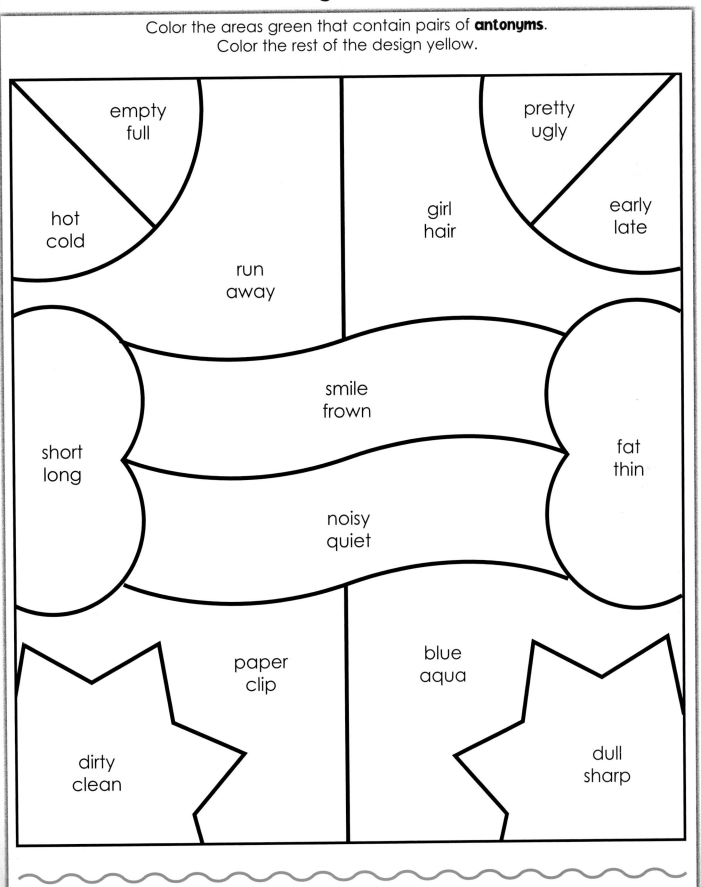

Measure Sense

Using the chart, circle the measurement choice that is most reasonable.

STANDARD LENGTH
12 in. = 1 ft.
3 ft. = 1 yd.
5,280 ft. = 1 mi.

STANDARD LENGTH
Inch (in.): the diameter of a quarter
Foot (ft.): from your shoulder to elbow
Yard (yd.): length of a teacher's desk
Mile (mi.): a short car ride

A. length of a fooball field	**B.** width of a math book	**C.** height of a fence	**D.** height of a desk
100 yd. 100 mi.	8 in. 8 ft.	4 in. 4 ft.	2 in. 2 ft.
E. height of a doorway	**F.** width of your wrist	**G.** length of a parking lot	**H.** length of your foot
7 in. 7 ft.	3 in. 3 ft.	50 yd. 50 mi.	7 in. 7 ft.

Conversion Excursion

Use the conversion chart to complete the statements below.

Standard Length

12 in.	=	1 ft.
3 ft.	=	1 yd.
5,280 ft.	=	1 mi.
1,760 yd.	=	1 mi.

24 in. = _____ ft.

6 yd. = _____ ft.

12 ft. = _____ yd.

10,560 ft. = _____ mi.

36 in. = _____ ft.

60 in. = _____ ft.

48 in. = _____ ft.

1 yd. = _____ in.

5 yd. = _____ ft.

36 ft. = _____ yd.

1 ft. = _____ in.

10 ft. = _____ in.

Remove pages 139–142. Cut along dashed lines. Staple pages in order.

Flying Disc Science

1

Have you ever wondered what makes a flying disc fly? How is it that an object with such a simple shape can travel through the air for so far and for so long? After all, it's just a lightweight plastic disc.

But look closer. You will notice that the sides are rounded and the top of it is raised. Some of the same ideas behind the design of a flying disc can be found in a sketch of an airplane wing. Don't worry—you won't need a pilot's license to throw a flying disc. But it won't hurt to know why the designs of both objects are similar.

3

Did you know that more flying discs are sold each year than footballs, baseballs, and basketballs combined? How is it that a simple round disc could bring so much fun to so many people?

Perhaps it's because the flying disc isn't as simple as it may seem. Even its history is complicated. The original design came from pie tins made by the Frisbie Baking Company in 1871. These tins started to turn up on college campuses, but not just because they contained delicious pies. The students, after enjoying a tasty dessert, discovered that if you tossed a tin in just the right way, with a sharp twist of the wrist, the tin could soar for many yards. It became a fun, new toy.

Then, in 1948, Walter Morrison and Warren Franscioni decided to make a plastic version of the Frisbie pie tin. They called the toy the Pluto Platter because the disc looked like a UFO. When the toy company Wham-O purchased the invention, they renamed it the Frisbee®. Ten years later, "Frisbee®" was a household word in the United States.

THRUST

A flying disc throw is really a contest of forces. A **force** pushes or pulls an object in some direction. Some forces try to keep the Frisbee moving through the air. Others try to bring it to a stop.

The first force that acts on a flying disc is called **thrust**. Thrust is a force that pushes on an object. When you throw a flying disc, you're pushing it through the air. A jet engine does the same thing to an airplane. It pushes the plane into the air and keeps it there.

So without thrust, the plastic disc wouldn't move at all. There's not much point in having a flying disc if you're just going to let it sit there.

The thrust applied to a flying disc is opposed by another force called **air resistance**. It pushes back against the flying disc, reducing the amount of thrust. Have you ever gone for a bike ride and noticed the air beating against your face and messing up your hair? The same thing happens to the plastic disc. Air pushes against it, slowing the disc down as it flies through it.

This is one of the reasons why the edges of the plastic disc are round. The air rolls over the flying disc a lot easier this way than if the edges were straight up and down. The same is true for the airplane wing. See how the front of it is smooth and curved? This shape makes it easier for the plane to slide through the air.

5

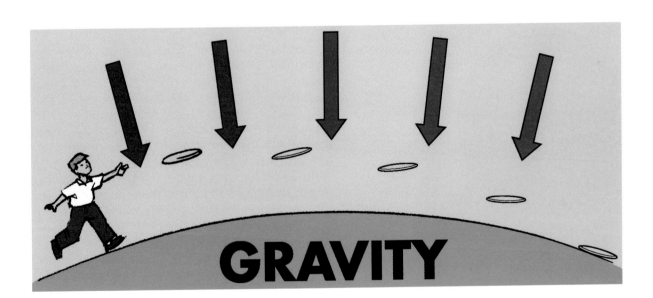

So why doesn't the flying disc just float off into space since air is constantly pushing it upwards? It's because the force of **gravity** is pulling down on the plastic disc, too. Earth's gravity pulls all the objects on its surface toward its center. That's why we don't float off into space.

If no one catches a tossed plastic disc, eventually gravity will win and the flying disc will land on the ground. If there were no such thing as gravity, you could throw a flying disc for a very long way.

7

The flying disc's curved sides and top cause another force to help its flight. This force is called **lift**. Just as it sounds, this force lifts an object into the air and lets it soar.

Because of the disc's rounded sides, air passing across the top of it has a longer distance to travel than it does along its flat bottom. To catch up with the air moving below it, the air on top has to move faster. When the air speeds up, it has less time to push down on the flying disc's top. The slower air beneath the flat bottom of the disc has more time to push up on it. And so, the air lifts the plastic disc.

The same thing happens to an airplane wing. The air beneath the wing pushes up on it, keeping the plane in the air. Without lift, air travel would not be possible.

6

Have you ever had trouble throwing a flying disc straight? The reason for this is that you might not be putting enough spin on it. In order to throw a flying disc, you have to snap your wrist. This causes the plastic disc to spin rapidly as it flies through the air. Much like a toy top, the spinning keeps the disc from wobbling and flying in all kinds of crazy directions. If you don't snap your wrist when you toss it, your flying disc will probably crash to the ground soon after you let it go. That's not much fun for the person waiting to catch it.

It is also important to hold the disc level when you toss it. If you don't, you'll see your flying disc curving away from the friend you've tossed it to. Try keeping the disc level and see how that works.

Of course, throwing a flying disc isn't as simple as it looks, but once you learn how to do it, your next trip to the beach or park will be a lot more fun!

8

Spelling Assessment

Read each group of words. Mark the word that is **not** spelled correctly.

1. □ several
   □ skirt
   □ spiret
   □ strain
   □ torn

2. □ yawn
   □ yourselves
   □ wow
   □ wastte
   □ twin

3. □ tomato
   □ sword
   □ stole
   □ sparkel
   □ sixth

4. □ serve
   □ ruber
   □ rear
   □ prepare
   □ pinch

5. □ pad
   □ neklace
   □ mess
   □ knife
   □ hero

6. □ footprint
   □ fern
   □ dozzen
   □ degree
   □ create

7. □ coast
   □ cellar
   □ broom
   □ behav
   □ attention

8. □ gloom
   □ footstep
   □ envelope
   □ drag
   □ creeture

9. □ cent
   □ belly
   □ attick
   □ address
   □ account

10. □ avenue
    □ bufalo
    □ colorful
    □ croak
    □ dentist

11. □ dredful
    □ event
    □ fifty
    □ forward
    □ goodbye

12. □ guy
    □ history
    □ ink
    □ lace
    □ lowwer

13. □ pale
    □ sadle
    □ shady
    □ slam
    □ stray

14. □ tan
    □ tough
    □ undergroun
    □ warmth
    □ tin

15. □ mist
    □ nibble
    □ place
    □ pitcker
    □ princess

16. □ rust
    □ skunk
    □ spit
    □ tame
    □ yeserday

17. □ warn
    □ twice
    □ tip
    □ stirr
    □ sip

18. □ rowboat
    □ readder
    □ pill
    □ package
    □ neat

19. □ merry
    □ lood
    □ herd
    □ guide
    □ glitter

20. □ ache
    □ awakken
    □ birdhouse
    □ buggy
    □ charm

21. □ comb
    □ crocoodile
    □ department
    □ examine
    □ gym

22. □ actual
    □ acorn
    □ aim
    □ awerd
    □ birth

23. □ chatter
    □ comfort
    □ crooke
    □ depend
    □ drift

24. □ example
    □ fought
    □ haircut
    □ inssist
    □ laid

25. □ lung
    □ mister
    □ noble
    □ plannet
    □ sadness

26. □ shagy
    □ slant
    □ split
    □ tangle
    □ tour

27. □ sort
    □ single
    □ Septeber
    □ ray
    □ lizard

28. □ helpless
    □ geust
    □ glide
    □ football
    □ female

Narrative Passage

Read the story, then read each question. Read all the answers and mark the space for the answer you think is right. Mark NH (not here) if the answer can not be figured out from the given information.

Lillian slid lower in her chair. She was almost under her desk. If she could just disappear, maybe the teacher wouldn't call on her. Lillian was prepared. She loved to read and had finished the book two weeks ago. She also liked to write, so the book report was no problem. Lillian did not want to read her report to the class. Her stomach felt sick and her face got hot every time she thought about standing up in front of all those children. The teacher called Lillian's name. Lillian slowly stood up and shuffled to the front of the room. She thought about Sam, a character in her book. If only she could be as brave as he was. Suddenly, Lillian knew what to do! She closed her eyes and pretended she was Sam. She told Sam's story, just as if it had happened to her. When she was finished, Lillian opened her eyes and looked at the class in front of her. They were clapping wildly because she had given such a good report! The teacher was very happy and gave Lillian an A+ on her report. Lillian was happy, too!

1. Why was Lillian trying to hide under her desk?
○ **She did not want to give the report.**
○ **She was not feeling well.**
○ **She always hid under there.**
○ **NH**

2. Lillian was afraid of something. What was she afraid of?
○ **reading aloud**
○ **standing up in front of the class**
○ **her teacher**
○ **NH**

3. Why did the teacher make Lillian give the report?
○ **She didn't like Lillian.**
○ **It was Lillian's turn to report.**
○ **She wanted Lillian to be brave.**
○ **NH**

4. How did Lillian help herself get through the report?
○ **She pretended she was at home.**
○ **She pretended to be brave.**
○ **She pretended to be Sam.**
○ **NH**

5. What words from the story give clues about how Lillian felt giving book reports in front of the class?
○ **brave, pretended, wildly**
○ **happy, character, problem**
○ **disappear, sick, shuffled**
○ **NH**

6. What grade did Lillian get for her report?
○ **A+**
○ **E+**
○ **A**
○ **NH**

Vocabulary Assessment

Read the first part of the sentence and look at the underlined word or phrase. Choose the word that means about the same thing as the underlined word or phrase. Mark the correct answer.

1. To make something look larger is to . . .
   - ○ shovel
   - ○ lighten
   - ○ magnify

2. To save something is to . . .
   - ○ preserve
   - ○ outwit
   - ○ lasso

3. Something that is strong and solid is . . .
   - ○ hoarse
   - ○ sturdy
   - ○ harmful

4. Something evil or bad is . . .
   - ○ wicked
   - ○ mischief
   - ○ slender

5. To surprise greatly is to . . .
   - ○ astonish
   - ○ cradle
   - ○ involve

6. To sort or put things into categories is to . . .
   - ○ educate
   - ○ insult
   - ○ classify

7. A strong feeling of wanting to know or learn is . . .
   - ○ lark
   - ○ curiosity
   - ○ harmony

8. Something that has no feeling is . . .
   - ○ society
   - ○ mixture
   - ○ numb

9. A smell or odor is a . . .
   - ○ humor
   - ○ dipper
   - ○ scent

10. A person visiting a new place is a . . .
    - ○ twitch
    - ○ runaway
    - ○ tourist

11. To move forward is to . . .
    - ○ advance
    - ○ salute
    - ○ skim

12. Something that has a strong, unpleasant taste is . . .
    - ○ fiery
    - ○ bitter
    - ○ crimson

13. The power to work or be active is . . .
    - ○ energy
    - ○ glimpse
    - ○ display

14. A motion made with the arms is a . . .
    - ○ freckle
    - ○ gesture
    - ○ custodian

15. To move a little is to . . .
    - ○ budge
    - ○ dimple
    - ○ lend

16. To worry is to be . . .
    - ○ concerned
    - ○ lame
    - ○ eerie

17. A strong dislike that makes you feel sick is called . . .
    - ○ length
    - ○ disgust
    - ○ reflection

18. Something very good is . . .
    - ○ shatter
    - ○ modest
    - ○ fantastic

19. A person who tells the truth is . . .
    - ○ hasty
    - ○ honest
    - ○ horrified

20. To want what others have is to be . . .
    - ○ beaten
    - ○ classical
    - ○ jealous

21. A smell is an . . .
    - ○ diagram
    - ○ odor
    - ○ crime

Place Value with Large Numbers

Use the given number to find the place values. The first one has been done for you.

1. The number is: **7,320,194.685**

   a. Name the digit in the tens place. _____ q _____

   b. Name the digit in the tenths place. _____

   c. Name the digit in the millions place. _____

   d. Name the digit in the ones place. _____

   e. In what place value is the digit 0? _____

   f. In what place is the digit 2? _____

   g. In what place value is the digit 3? _____

   h. In what place value is the digit 5? _____

2. The number is: **8,635.147**

   a. Name the digit in the hundreds place. _____

   b. Name the digit in the hundredths place. _____

   c. Name the digit in the thousands place. _____

   d. Name the digit in the tenths place. _____

   e. Name the number that is one hundred more. _____

   f. Name the number that is one thousand less. _____

   g. Name the number that is one-hundredth less. _____

   h. Name the number that is one more. _____

3. The number is: **1,320,796.485**

   a. Name the digit in the millions place. _____

   b. Name the digit in the ones place. _____

   c. Name the digit in the thousandths place. _____

   d. Name the digit in the ten thousands place. _____

   e. Name the number that is ten thousand less. _____

   f. Name the number that is one-thousandth more. _____

   g. Name the number that is one less. _____

   h. Name the number that is one million more. _____

Answer Key

Page 16

Matching Vowel Sounds

Draw a line to connect each word in the first column with a word in the second column that has the same vowel sound.

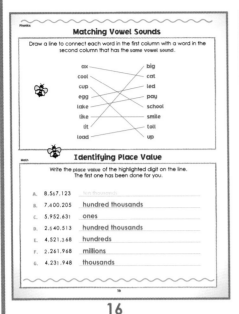

ax	big
cool	cat
cup	led
egg	pay
lake	school
like	smile
lit	toll
load	up

Identifying Place Value

Write the place value of the highlighted digit on the line. The first one has been done for you.

A. 8,567,123 — ten thousands
B. 7,400,205 — hundred thousands
C. 5,952,631 — ones
D. 2,540,513 — hundred thousands
E. 4,521,368 — hundreds
F. 2,261,968 — millions
G. 4,231,948 — thousands

Page 17

Standard Form Notation

Write each number in standard form.

A. 500 + 90 + 6 = 596
B. 2,000 + 400 + 60 + 7 = 2,467
C. 40,000 + 3,000 + 800 + 20 + 1 = 43,821
D. 200,000 + 50,000 + 7,000 + 10 + 4 = 257,014
E. Write your own. — answers will vary

Dictionary Pronunciation

Listen to the vowel sounds in each word below, then draw a line to connect each word with its dictionary pronunciation.

dream	(at)
knot	(pik'el)
shirt	(rit)
crew	(shurt)
officer	(kom'it)
tense	(drēm)
write	(kroo)
mermaid	(mur'mad)
pickle	(not)
eight	(o'fi sar)
comet	(tens)

Page 18

Beginning Consonant Blends

Look at the consonant blends in the box below. Write a blend on each line to form a word that matches one of the pictures. Draw a line from the word to its picture.

cl   dr   sc   sk   sn   st

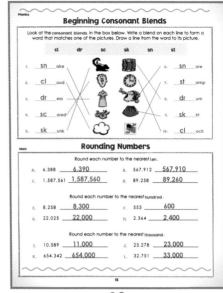

1. sn ake
2. cl oud
3. dr ess
4. sc ared
5. sk unk
6. sn ore
7. st amp
8. dr um
9. sk irt
10. cl ock

Rounding Numbers

Round each number to the nearest ten.

A. 6,388 — 6,390
B. 567,912 — 567,910
C. 1,587,561 — 1,587,560
D. 89,258 — 89,260

Round each number to the nearest hundred.

E. 8,258 — 8,300
F. 553 — 600
G. 22,025 — 22,000
H. 2,364 — 2,400

Round each number to the nearest thousand.

I. 10,589 — 11,000
J. 23,278 — 23,000
K. 654,342 — 654,000
L. 32,751 — 33,000

Page 19

Understanding Place Value

Write the place value of the highlighted digit on the line. The first one has been done for you.

A. 3,921 — hundreds
B. 1,572 — thousands
C. 2,463 — thousands
D. 5,761 — tens
E. 4,984 — tens
F. 1,756 — hundreds
G. 6,357 — tens
H. 6,852 — ones

Complete the Sentence

Use the words from the word list to complete the sentences below.

Word List: insists, blend, borrow, dangerous, entire, proud, amazing, fond

1. The acrobats at the circus do **amazing** tricks.
2. Jan is **fond** of her new classmate, Diana.
3. When you **blend** blue and yellow, you get green.
4. Mom always **insists** that I wear my seat belt.
5. Playing in the street can be **dangerous**.
6. I was **proud** when I won first prize.
7. May I **borrow** your eraser?
8. Sarah drank the **entire** carton of milk.

Page 20

Ending Consonant Blends

Choose a consonant blend from the word list to complete a different word on each line.

Answers will vary.

Word List: tt, sp, mp, nd, nk, nt, st

1. ba____
2. la____
3. la____
4. si____
5. ca____
6. da____
7. da____
8. de____
9. ba____
10. si____
11. tru____
12. tru____
13. ca____
14. da____
15. cri____

Understanding Place Value

Write the place value of the highlighted digit in the box.

A. 47,629 — ones
B. 35,116 — hundreds
C. 59,024 — thousands
D. 23,199 — tens
E. 98,965 — thousands
F. 78,620 — ten thousands
G. 83,456 — ten thousands
H. 19,201 — thousands

Page 21

A Friendly Letter

Write a letter to your favorite actor or actress. Include all five parts of a friendly letter. Remember to put a comma after the greeting and closing.

Letters will vary.

Addressing an Envelope

Address the envelope below using the information given.

The sender is:
Mr. Fred Barrow
216 Dawson Drive
Ogden, UT 66065

The receiver is:
Ms. Carla George
22 W. 42nd Street
Tampa, FL 21563

Mr. Fred Barrow
216 Dawson Drive
Ogden, UT 66065

Ms. Carla George
22 W. 42nd Street
Tampa, FL 21563

Page 22

Identifying Types of Stories

Read each title below. Write F on the line if you believe the story is fiction. NF if you think it is nonfiction, or B if you think it is a biography.

F 1. Kelly's Rainbow Zebra
NF 2. Life in Jamestown
NF 3. How Cars Are Made
F 4. We Rode on a Unicorn
NF 5. Plants of North America
B 6. The Life of Albert Einstein
F 7. My Trip to Mars
B 8. Lincoln, the Sixteenth President
F 9. Georgie, the Singing Monkey
B 10. All about Susan B. Anthony
NF 11. The Battles of the Civil War
F 12. The 10,000-Year-Old Woman

Fiction: a story that is made-up or is not factual
Nonfiction: a true or factual story
Biography: a story about a real person's life

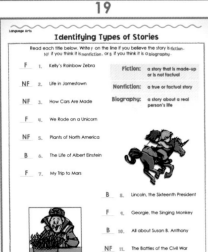

Page 23

Silent Letters

Draw a circle around the silent letter or letters in each word.

1. know
2. comb
3. kneel
4. light
5. ghastly
6. write
7. gnaw
8. wrap
9. gnat
10. knife
11. home
12. knock
13. knot
14. thumb
15. climb
16. tomb
17. wrench
18. knit
19. dough
20. knight
21. knee
22. gnu
23. wrist
24. marl

Two-Digit Addition

Circle the even answers. Draw a square around the odd answers.

A. 86 + 45 = 131
B. 62 + 95 = 157
C. 81 + 55 = 136
D. 37 + 87 = 124
E. 64 + 56 = 120
F. 50 + 58 = 108
G. 65 + 70 = 135
H. 98 + 14 = 112
I. 88 + 58 = 146
J. 94 + 21 = 115
K. 54 + 87 = 141
L. 54 + 64 = 118
M. 73 + 15 = 88
N. 82 + 41 = 123
O. 33 + 45 = 78

Page 24

Abbreviations

Write the correct abbreviation for each on the line beside it. Use the abbreviations word list.

Apartment — Apt.
Avenue — Ave.
Boulevard — Blvd.
Building — Bldg.
Railroad — RR
Road — Rd.
dozen — dz.
Junior — Jr.
centimeter — cm
Department — Dept.
teaspoon — tsp.
hour — hr.

Word List: Bldg., cm, tsp., Apt., Jr., Ave., Blvd., Dept., hr., RR, dz., Rd.

Classifying

Read the words in each box. Circle the word that does not belong with the others.

seven	forty		July	December
fork	sixteen		Monday	February

flour	sugar		movie	letter
milk	kitchen		magazine	book

owl	kangaroo		black	house
cantaloupe	wolf		orange	yellow

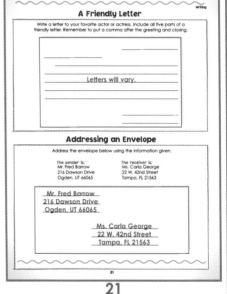

147

Answer Key

Following Directions

Reading Comprehension

Follow the directions to draw a picture in the box.

1. Draw a tree with four branches and orange and red leaves in the bottom left corner.
2. Draw a yellow half moon in the upper right corner.
3. Draw a brown fence across the bottom.
4. Draw four gray cats on the fence.
5. Draw six dark clouds in the sky.
6. Draw one owl on a branch of the tree.
7. Draw five black birds flying in the sky.
8. Add any other details you wish.

Pictures will vary but should follow the directions given.

25

Break the Code

Math

Find the sums. Write the letter next to each problem on the correct lines below to read the coded message.

96 + 58	56 + 86	79 + 38	86 + 27	38 + 87	64 + 83
(I) 154	(V) 142	(D) 117	(E) 113	(K) 125	(D) 147

89 + 47	58 + 62	73 + 49	86 + 76	69 + 52	77 + 54
(U) 136	(G) 120	(A) 122	(Y) 162	(W) 121	(R) 131

V E R Y   G O O D   W O R K
142 131 162   120 117 117 147   121 147 131 125

Categories of Words

Reading Comprehension

Circle the three words that belong together in a category.

1. (golf) (lawyer) (artist) (doctor)
2. (train) car (airplane) glove
3. (lungs) (brain) (heart) food
4. Canada (Texas) (Virginia) (Florida)
5. (necklace) (ring) balloon (bracelet)
6. (happy) (grumpy) (embarrassed) laughter

26

Alphabetical Order

Language Arts

Write numbers in front of the words in each group to put them in alphabetical order.

A.		B.		C.	
6	king	1	toast	1	egg
2	keen	2	toffee	3	elephant
4	kernel	4	told	6	ensemble
7	knee	5	tomorrow	4	elf
3	keep	6	total	2	electric
5	kind	3	together	5	ending
1	kangaroo	7	tough	7	especially

Using Math Symbols <, >, or =

Math

Solve each problem. Print the answer next to the correct letter at the bottom. Place the correct symbol (<, >, or =) in the circle.

A. 22 + 35 = 57   B. 60 + 39 = 99   C. 50 + 31 = 81
D. 63 + 20 = 83   E. 10 + 3 = 13   F. 50 + 25 = 75
G. 77 + 7 = 84   H. 60 + 21 = 81   I. 12 + 30 = 42

57 (<) 84   81 (=) 81
(A)   (G)   (C)   (H)

99 (>) 42   75 (>) 13
(B)   (I)   (F)   (E)

83 (<) 84   57 (<) 84
(D)   (G)   (A)   (G)

27

Cloze

Reading Comprehension

Read the story below. Many words are missing. Fill in the blanks with words from the word list.

Randy loved to paint. He liked to paint with his fingers **when** he was little. He would paint on **paper**. He would paint on tables. Once he **even** painted on the living room wall. Randy's **parents** were not happy with his painting. They **begged** him to play ball or ride his **bicycle** but Randy only wanted to paint. When **Randy** was older, he helped the neighbors paint **their** house. He painted a huge but beautiful **flower** on the front of their house. The **neighbors** did not want a huge, beautiful flower **painted** on the front of their house. Randy **lost** that job! Today Randy is very happy. **He** is a famous painter. Now his parents **love** his painting. And the neighbors wish they still had the flower on the front of their house.

Word List
begged
bicycle
even
flower
He
lost
love
neighbors
painted
paper
parents
Randy
their
when

Three-Digit Addition

Math

Add to solve each problem.

A.	B.	C.	D.
486 + 514 1,000	237 + 185 422	902 + 404 1,306	375 + 612 987

E.	F.	G.	H.
842 + 254 1,096	951 + 726 1,677	33 76 + 54 163	45 48 + 85 178

28

Addition with Decimals

Math

Add to solve each problem.

A.	B.	C.	D.
3.5 + 8.2 11.7	7.9 + 3.1 11.0	9.0 + 4.8 13.8	49.5 + 52.4 101.9

E.	F.	G.	H.
7.03 + 7.85 14.88	3.25 + 4.94 8.19	8.03 + 5.13 13.16	49.6 + 31.2 80.8

Syllables

Language Arts

Read the animal names below. Count the number of syllables in each name. Print the number of syllables in the box.

rabbit	2	snake	1	elephant	3
monkey	2	lion	2	giraffe	2
flamingo	3	manatee	3	dinosaur	3
koala	3	wolverine	3	dolphin	2
whale	1	aardvark	2	emu	2

29

Writing Paragraphs

Writing

Read the title and main idea of the paragraph. Write your own details.

Title of paragraph: My Best Friend

Main Idea: My best friend is someone special.

Details:
1.
2.
3.
4.

Answers will vary.

Retell the Main Idea: I am glad I have such a great friend.

Use the information above to write a paragraph. Include the main idea and details, then retell the main idea. Indent the first sentence. Use capital letters and periods. Remember to title the paragraph.

Answers will vary.

30

Days of the Week Abbreviations

Language Arts

Write the **abbreviation** for each day of the week. Then find each word in the word search below.

1. Sunday — **Sun.**
2. Thursday — **Thurs.**
3. Friday — **Fri.**
4. Saturday — **Sat.**
5. Monday — **Mon.**
6. Wednesday — **Wed.**
7. Tuesday — **Tues.**

```
M O N D A Y R G H W U
P T O L G F E A C E Y
D H S U N D A Y F D A
I U W J S D P A N S Z
S R M T W T F S P E X
S S J F M A M F D S C
Y D J J S A O R P D E
G A N D O T F I P A L
F Y F T U E S D A Y Y
H I O N E I S A O E J
S A T U R D A Y G L P
J M P Q W S L N T Y D
U E R L W T F V Y J A
X I L W R V A O P W M
```

31

Context Clues

Reading Comprehension

One word has been highlighted in each sentence below. There are two definitions given for each word. Decide which meaning is correct by reading the sentence and thinking about how the word is used. Circle the correct meaning.

1. The ball was broken, so the bucket of water was difficult to lift.
   a. throw water out   (b. the handle of a pail)
2. The princess had a grand time at the ball last night.
   (a. a dance)   b. a round object
3. Joe left before I could tell him good-bye.
   a. the opposite of right   (b. went away)
4. Jack had a fit when his brother broke his new bicycle.
   a. suitable   (b. an attack)
5. The group became grave when they saw the danger they were in.
   (a. serious)   b. a place of burial

Three-Digit Addition

Math

Time yourself. How fast can you complete the problems?

A.
410 + 291 701	737 + 288 1,015	426 + 497 923	166 + 617 783	404 + 395 799	259 + 450 709	272 + 438 710

B.
357 + 417 774	519 + 170 689	834 + 196 1,030	313 + 488 801	558 + 184 742	687 + 139 826	901 + 149 1,050

Time: _____   Number correct: _____

32

Reading a Bar Graph

Math

The bar graph below shows how many boxes of cookies were sold at Discovery Elementary School over an eight-week period. Use the graph to answer the questions.

Boxes of Cookies Sold at Discovery Elementary School

Number of Boxes Sold (vertical axis: 0, 10, 20, 30, 40, 50, 60, 70)
Week (horizontal axis: 1–8)

A. What was the total number of boxes sold during the eight-week sale? **250**
B. During which two weeks were the same number of boxes sold? **4 and 7**
C. How many more boxes were sold during week 6 than week 7? **20**
D. How many fewer boxes were sold during week 8 than week 2? **10**
E. How many boxes were sold during week 3? **0** What do you think might have happened? **Answers will vary.**

33

Answer Key

Three-Digit Column Addition

Add to solve each problem.

A.	B.	C.	D.
402	800	257	589
715	240	946	456
+ 513	+ 912	+ 178	+ 981
1,630	1,952	1,381	2,026

E.	F.	G.	H.
643	321	814	136
285	419	901	912
133	444	121	978
+ 341	+ 750	+ 215	+ 222
1,402	1,934	2,051	2,248

Riddles

Twenty white horses up a red hill.
Now they chomp. Now they stomp.
Now they stand still.
What are they?

The words in the box make a riddle. They have a hidden meaning. Can you guess what the riddle is about? The answer is teeth! There are twenty white teeth in your mouth. The red hill is your gums. As you talk, they move up and down as if they are chomping and stomping. When you finish talking, they "stand still."

Riddles give a symbolic meaning to things. They have been used for thousands of years. In ancient times, wise people would often answer questions with riddles. It was believed that knowledge was precious, or of great value, and should not be given to everyone. If a person could solve a riddle, he was smart enough to know the answer.

1. What is the main idea of this story?
   a. Riddles are used as symbols.
   b. Riddles have been used for many years.
   c. Riddles are hard to figure out.

2. What is a riddle? Words that give symbolic meaning to something

3. The word precious means:
   a. a lot of money
   b. meaning
   c. valuable

4. Instead of giving an answer, why did wise people speak in riddles?
   Only smart or wise people could figure out the answers.

34

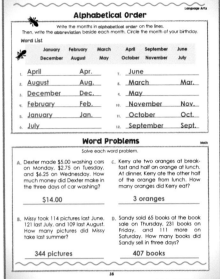

Alphabetical Order

Write the months in alphabetical order on the lines. Then, write the abbreviation beside each month. Circle the month of your birthday.

Word List

January	February	March	April	September	June
December	August	May	October	November	July

1. April — Apr.
2. August — Aug.
3. December — Dec.
4. February — Feb.
5. January — Jan.
6. July
7. June
8. March — Mar.
9. May
10. November — Nov.
11. October — Oct.
12. September — Sept.

Word Problems

Solve each word problem.

A. Dexter made $5.00 washing cars on Monday, $2.75 on Tuesday, and $6.25 on Wednesday. How much money did Dexter make in the three days of car washing?
$14.00

B. Missy took 114 pictures last June, 121 last July, and 109 last August. How many pictures did Missy take last summer?
344 pictures

C. Kerry ate two oranges at breakfast and half an orange at lunch. At dinner, Kerry ate the other half of the orange from lunch. How many oranges did Kerry eat?
3 oranges

D. Sandy sold 65 books at the book sale on Thursday, 231 more on Friday, and 111 more on Saturday. How many books did Sandy sell in three days?
407 books

35

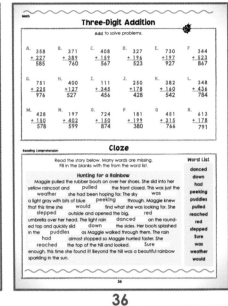

Three-Digit Addition

Add to solve problems.

A.	B.	C.	D.	E.	F.
358	371	408	327	730	344
+ 227	+ 389	+ 159	+ 196	+ 197	+ 523
585	760	567	523	927	867

G.	H.	I.	J.	K.	L.
751	400	111	250	382	348
+ 225	+ 127	+ 345	+ 178	+ 160	+ 436
976	527	456	428	542	784

M.	N.	O.	P.	Q.	R.
428	197	724	181	451	613
+ 150	+ 402	+ 150	+ 199	+ 315	+ 178
578	599	874	380	766	791

Cloze

Read the story below. Many words are missing. Fill in the blanks with the from the word list.

Hunting for a Rainbow

Maggie pulled the rubber boots on over her shoes. She slid into her yellow raincoat and **pulled** the front closed. This was just the **weather** she had been hoping for. The sky **was** a light gray with bits of blue **peeking** through. Maggie knew that at this time she **would** find what she was looking for. She **stepped** outside and opened the big **red** umbrella over her head. The light rain **danced** on the round-ed top and quickly slid **down** the sides. Her boots splashed in the **puddles** as Maggie walked through them. The rain **had** almost stopped so Maggie hurried faster. She **reached** the top of the hill and looked. **Sure** enough, this time she found it! Beyond the hill was a beautiful rainbow sparkling in the sun.

Word List
danced
down
had
peeking
puddles
pulled
reached
red
stepped
Sure
was
weather
would

36

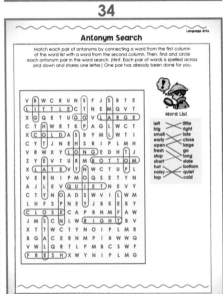

Antonym Search

Match each pair of antonyms by connecting a word from the first column of the word list with a word from the second column. Then, find and circle each antonym pair in the word search. (Hint: Each pair of words is spelled across and down and shares one letter.) One pair has already been done for you.

```
V B W C R U N S F J S B T E
L I T T L E C T N E M Q V T
X G Q E T U G O V L A R G E
C T H W R T K P A G L W C T
C O L D A S B Y M L W T I
C Y T J N E H S R I P L M H
V R W X Y L O N G E D H T J
Z Y E V T U R M B O T T O M
X L A T E Y N W C T U P L
V E R N I P M O Q S E T Y N
A J L E V Q U I E T N E V Y
L H F S P N E J J B K E B Y
C L O S E C A P R N M F A W
J M S C N L W R I G H T B V
X T T W C T Y N O I P L M R
B G A C E R N M P I B W W Q
V W L Q R T L M B C S W F
F R E S H X W Y N I P L M G
```

Word List
left — little
big — right
small — late
early — close
open — large
fresh — go
stop — long
short — stale
hot — bottom
noisy — quiet
top — cold

41

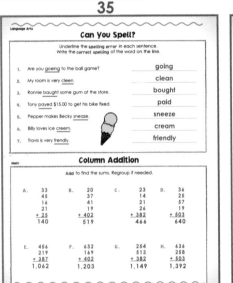

Can You Spell?

Underline the spelling error in each sentence. Write the correct spelling of the word on the line.

1. Are you goeing to the ball game? — going
2. My room is very cleen. — clean
3. Ronnie baught some gum at the store. — bought
4. Tony payed $15.00 to get his bike fixed. — paid
5. Pepper makes Becky sneaze. — sneeze
6. Billy loves ice creem. — cream
7. Travis is very frendly. — friendly

Column Addition

Add to find the sums. Regroup if needed.

A.	B.	C.	D.
33	20	23	36
45	37	14	25
16	41	21	19
21	19	26	19
+ 25	+ 402	+ 382	+ 603
140	519	466	640

E.	F.	G.	H.
456	632	254	636
219	169	513	258
+ 387	+ 402	+ 382	+ 503
1,062	1,203	1,149	1,392

42

Alphabetical Order

Write the words from the word list in alphabetical order on the lines.

1. asteroid
2. astronauts
3. Earth
4. Jupiter
5. Mars
6. Mercury
7. moon
8. Neptune
9. planet
10. Pluto
11. satellite
12. Saturn
13. shuttle
14. universe
15. Uranus
16. Venus

Word List
Mars, Venus, Mercury, Jupiter, Uranus, Neptune, satellite, universe, planet, shuttle, Earth, asteroid, Saturn, Pluto, moon, astronauts

43

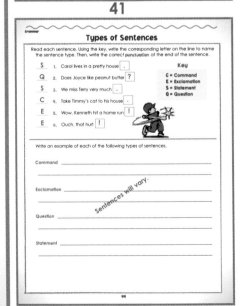

Types of Sentences

Read each sentence. Using the key, write the corresponding letter on the line to name the sentence type. Then, write the correct punctuation at the end of the sentence.

S 1. Carol lives in a pretty house **.**
Q 2. Does Joyce like peanut butter **?**
S 3. We miss Terry very much **.**
C 4. Take Timmy's cat to his house **.**
E 5. Wow, Kenneth hit a home run **!**
E 6. Ouch, that hurt **!**

Key
C = Command
E = Exclamation
S = Statement
Q = Question

Write an example of each of the following types of sentences.

Command _____

Exclamation _____

Sentences will vary.

Question _____

Statement _____

44

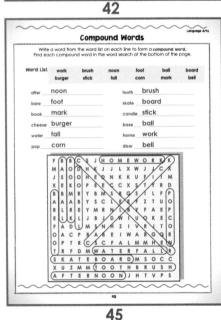

Compound Words

Write a word from the word list on each line to form a compound word. Find each compound word in the word search at the bottom of the page.

Word List
work, brush, noon, foot, ball, board
burger, stick, fall, corn, mark, bell

after — noon
bare — foot
book — mark
cheese — burger
water — fall
pop — corn

tooth — brush
skate — board
candle — stick
base — ball
home — work
door — bell

```
F B B C J H O M E W O R K K
M A O D H K J J L X W J C A
J S O O H E O N K K U E I M
E K B Y H E E C C X T W Y T
B B M R Y B M S R Q S L F P
A A A B Y S C L E F Z T U O
R L K Y M R N L Y F A E P
E L K L J B J D W U O K E C
F A D L M S N J Z I V R I T
O A C P R A B E I W A B G O
O P T R C S C F A L M M H E N
T R F D M W A T E R F A L L R
S K A T E B O A R D M S O C C
X U Z M M T O O T H B R U S H
A F T E R N O O N J H T V P S
```

45

Building Vocabulary

Beth wants to be a paramedic and she practices on her dog, Gumbo. Read the story to see how Gumbo feels about all of this. Then, read each of the five sentences. Write the letter for the best answer on the line.

Good Old Gumbo . . .

No dog was ever as patient as Gumbo. Just ask Beth. She is his owner. Beth has put Gumbo through a great deal in his young life. He's been a model for assorted doll clothes. He's retrieved baseballs from under thick hedges. Now Gumbo is a model again. This time it's for splints and bandages.

Beth is learning all about first aid. She hopes to be a paramedic one day. She thinks helping people would be a good thing. She wants to practice every bandage and splint on Gumbo.

After only five minutes, Gumbo has become disturbed. He doesn't think being wrapped up is much fun. He decides that he'd better do something immediately. He has heard the saying, "being all tied up." Gumbo wants to get out of this while he's still can!

B 1. The word assorted means:
   a. tired b. mixed c. hungry d. distant

D 2. The word retrieved means:
   a. bought b. made c. begged d. brought back

A 3. The word disturbed means:
   a. upset b. soft c. silly d. loud

A 4. The word immediately means:
   a. now b. inside c. under d. never

D 5. A word in the story that is a synonym of bound is:
   a. owner b. rescue c. tied d. wrapped

Practice New Words
On a separate sheet of paper, write one sentence using each of these words:

assorted   retrieved   disturbed   immediately

46

Answer Key

Main Idea

The **main idea** of a paragraph is its central thought or topic. Read each paragraph. Read the three phrases under each paragraph. Decide which one tells the main idea. Write the letter of that phrase on the line.

B 1. Gary and Fritz have been writing to each other for four years. Gary lives in Indiana and Fritz lives in Germany. Gary looks forward to Fritz's letters. Fritz usually sends at least one picture and sometimes he sends extra German stamps for Gary's collection. Gary and Fritz both hope that they can meet someday. They feel as if they know each other already.

a. Pictures from Germany   b. Gary's German pen pal   c. Gary's friend

C 2. Mary has been blind all of her life. She has gone to special schools to learn to do things for herself. Her best friend Katy is not blind. Katy and Mary help each other. Mary is trying to teach Katy to read Braille. It is a special system of raised dots that lets Mary "read" the page. Katy isn't doing very well at all. Katy says that it is hard for her to "see" the letters with her fingers.

a. Learning to read   b. Understanding Braille   c. A special friendship

What's Missing?

Print the correct number in the box to complete each number sentence.

A. 2 + **11** = 13   B. 38 − **14** = 24   C. 28 − **13** = 15

D. 73 + **16** = 89   E. 40 − **7** = 33   F. 82 + **15** = 97

G. 55 + **18** = 73   H. 56 − **43** = 13   I. 19 + **14** = 33

J. 26 + **9** = 35   K. 28 − **9** = 19   L. 77 − **18** = 59

47

Two-Digit Subtraction Review

Calculate the following subtraction problems. Regroup as needed.

A. 15 − 5 = 10	B. 25 − 3 = 22	C. 10 − 2 = 28	D. 19 − 5 = 14	E. 14 − 5 = 9
F. 16 − 4 = 12	G. 19 − 2 = 17	H. 21 − 7 = 14	I. 40 − 5 = 35	J. 62 − 9 = 53
K. 28 − 16 = 12	L. 38 − 12 = 26	M. 42 − 7 = 35	N. 46 − 25 = 21	O. 28 − 14 = 14

Analogies

Fill in the blanks to complete the analogies.

1. A mouth is to taste as an eye is to **see**.
2. A person is to a house as a bear is to a **cave**.
3. An apple is to a tree as a watermelon is to a **vine**.
4. A kitten is to a cat as a puppy is to a **dog**.
5. An inch is to length as a pound is to **weight**.
6. A car is to a road as a boat is to **water**.
7. A whale is to water as an elephant is to **land**.

48

Nouns and Verbs

Read each sentence below. Underline each noun. Circle each verb.

1. Ryan and Cathy went to the museum.
2. Beverly washes the big, green car.
3. The big, black dog scared Chris.
4. Wanda lives in Georgia.
5. Don owns a large store.
6. The warm night was peaceful.
7. The girl was late for practice.
8. Brian put the blue sweater in the dryer.
9. Amber had fun at the park.

Regroup or Not to Regroup?

Subtract to find each difference.

A. 63 − 21 = 42	B. 45 − 25 = 20	C. 75 − 23 = 52	D. 33 − 11 = 22	E. 46 − 21 = 25
F. 32 − 15 = 17	G. 55 − 27 = 28	H. 90 − 42 = 48	I. 75 − 68 = 7	J. 35 − 16 = 19

49

Building Vocabulary

Davey has a new friend who keeps bothering him. Read the story to find out more. Then, read each of the five sentences. Write the letter for the best answer on the line.

A Fishing Friend

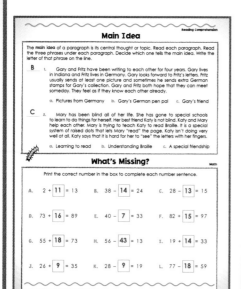

It all began last summer when Davey was fishing at his grandpa's farm. Suddenly, something odd occurred. A big head emerged from the water. The creature smiled and told Davey that his name was Clarence.

Clarence told Davey that he had always been alone and was tired of his solitude. He wanted a friend. Davey felt sorry for Clarence and tried his best to cheer him up.

Now it seems that Davey has a friend for life. There's just one problem: Clarence wants to be with Davey all the time. Davey can't go fishing alone anymore. He hopes Clarence will find another new friend soon. Davey would like some of his own solitude. He would also like to catch some fish. Few fish come around when Clarence is near!

D 1. The word occurred means:
a. pointed   b. painted   c. scraped   d. happened

B 2. The word emerged means:
a. fell in   b. came out   c. divided   d. twisted around

A 3. The word terrified means:
a. scared   b. rich   c. healthy   d. ripped

D 4. The word solitude means:
a. teacher   b. friends   c. leaving   d. being alone

A 5. A word in the story that is a synonym for desired is:
a. wanted   b. problem   c. cheer   d. destroyed

Practice New Words

On a separate sheet of paper, write one sentence using each of these words:

occurred   emerged   terrified   solitude

50

Beat the Clock (Double-Digit Subtraction)

Make several copies of this page. Time yourself every day for a week. Does your time improve? Does your accuracy increase?

A. 86 − 58 = 28	90 − 29 = 61	42 − 28 = 14	94 − 66 = 28	62 − 49 = 13	55 − 17 = 38	41 − 25 = 16
B. 75 − 17 = 58	47 − 18 = 29	40 − 29 = 11	61 − 23 = 38	54 − 38 = 16	81 − 27 = 54	67 − 38 = 29
C. 91 − 56 = 35	52 − 49 = 3	43 − 38 = 5	71 − 34 = 37	75 − 46 = 29	84 − 47 = 37	61 − 12 = 49
D. 93 − 75 = 18	84 − 19 = 65	82 − 73 = 9	84 − 37 = 47	66 − 48 = 18	75 − 27 = 48	54 − 39 = 15
E. 87 − 38 = 49	74 − 25 = 49	67 − 38 = 29	71 − 64 = 7	83 − 28 = 55	41 − 34 = 7	71 − 42 = 29

Time: _____   Number correct: _____

51

More Nouns and Verbs

Look at the words in the word list. Write the nouns on the building. Write the verbs on the rocket.

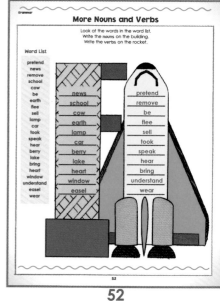

Word List

pretend, news, remove, school, cow, be, earth, flee, sell, lamp, car, took, speak, hear, berry, lake, bring, heart, window, understand, easel, wear

Nouns (building): news, school, cow, earth, lamp, car, berry, lake, heart, window, easel

Verbs (rocket): pretend, remove, be, flee, sell, took, speak, hear, bring, understand, wear

52

Plurals (-s or -es)

Add the correct ending (s or es) to make each word plural. Write the new words on the lines.

1. teacher — teachers
2. potato — potatoes
3. house — houses
4. kite — kites
5. class — classes
6. clown — clowns
7. box — boxes
8. handbook — handbooks
9. watch — watches
10. friend — friends
11. clock — clocks
12. computer — computers
13. couch — couches
14. carmel — carmels
15. fox — foxes

Adding & Subtracting with Decimals

Add or subtract to solve each problem.

A. 7.0 + 7.5 = 14.5	B. 9.2 − 4.1 = 5.1	C. 8.3 + 2.8 = 5.5
D. 23.5 − 16.3 = 7.2	E. 4.23 + 1.95 = 6.18	F. 6.35 − 4.96 = 1.39
G. 2.98 + 6.85 = 9.83	H. 96.3 − 21.4 = 74.9	I. 6.91 + 2.98 = 9.89

53

Story Problems

Solve each word problem.

A. Shannon bought 3 dozen eggs at the store. On the way home, she dropped the egg cartons and 13 of the eggs broke. How many unbroken eggs does Shannon now have? **36 − 13 = 23**

B. Dawn is allowed to swim in the pool for 60 minutes each day. If she has been swimming today for 25 minutes, how many more minutes does she have left in the pool? **60 − 25 = 35**

C. There were 937 students at Ridge Hill School. If 43 students missed school due to illness, how many students were at school? **937 − 43 = 894**

D. Phil's Used Car Lot had 142 cars to sell. If Phil sold 26 of the cars, how many did he have left to sell? **142 − 26 = 116**

E. Together, Cindy and Jim counted 221 cars on their road trip. Cindy counted 132 of the cars. How many cars did Jim count? **221 − 132 = 89**

Categories

Read each group of words or phrases. Choose the best category name from the box. Write the correct category under each list. The first one has been done for you.

Categories:
types of berries   summer clothing   things during a storm   baby animals   yellow things

1.	2.	3.	4.
A. sun	A. bathing suit	A. strawberry	A. foal
B. banana	B. sunglasses	B. raspberry	B. lamb
C. daisy	C. shorts	C. blackberry	C. chick
D. corn	D. sandals	D. blueberry	D. duckling
E. lemon	E. short-sleeved shirt	E. boysenberry	E. kitten

Category: yellow things   Category: summer clothing   Category: types of berries   Category: baby animals

54

Possessive Plurals

Make each highlighted word possessive by rewriting the word on the line and adding an apostrophe in the correct place.

1. That is Danas dollhouse. — Dana's
2. Craigs truck is very big. — Craig's
3. I like Sharons new green bicycle. — Sharon's
4. The childrens song was perfectly in tune. — children's
5. The two girls kites flew high in the sky. — girls'
6. The schools end-of-the-year picnic was fun. — school's
7. The trucks loud horn scared Barbara. — truck's
8. The actors costume was colorful. — actor's
9. I love to visit my grandmothers house. — grandmother's
10. The singers voices are beautiful. — singers'
11. Those dogs collars are green. — dogs'

Three- and Four-Digit Subtraction

Subtract to solve each problem. Circle the smallest answer. Draw a square around the largest answer.

A. 912 − 735 = 177	B. 583 − 321 = 262	C. 185 − 112 = 73	D. 635 − 504 = 131
E. 865 − 125 = 740	F. 999 − 428 = 571	G. 2,190 − 1,065 = 1,125	H. 5,948 − 2,374 = 3,574

55

Answer Key

Three-Digit Subtraction

Subtract to solve each problem. Circle all the even numbers.

A.
| 423 − 285 = (138) | 222 − 153 = 69 | 435 − 166 = 269 | 628 − 499 = 129 | 757 − 178 = 579 | 637 − 388 = 249 | 423 − 285 = (138) |

B.
| 326 − 285 = 41 | 972 − 609 = 363 | 685 − 246 = 439 | 518 − 329 = 189 | 741 − 362 = 379 | 438 − 258 = (180) | 371 − 283 = 88 |

C.
| 529 − 482 = 47 | 625 − 407 = (218) | 514 − 126 = (388) | 664 − 278 = 386 | 742 − 467 = 275 | 200 − 158 = (42) | 634 − 277 = 357 |

Adjectives

Underline the adjectives in each paragraph below.
The first adjective has been underlined for you.

1. I like _chocolate_ ice cream. Chocolate ice cream tastes good when it is hot outside. Unfortunately, chocolate ice cream makes a big, sticky mess. I solve this problem by eating my yummy, chocolate ice cream outside.

2. One sunny day, I found a white rabbit hopping in front of my house. I walked up to the frightened rabbit and talked to him. He finally calmed down and I picked him up. His soft fur tickled my hands. I took the sweet rabbit behind my house to the big forest. Waiting there for him was his happy mother. the two small rabbits hopped home together.

56

Persuasive Paragraph

You must convince your mom to let you go bowling.
Ask her, give your reasons, and then ask again.

Title of paragraph: _____

Question: May I _____

Reasons:
1.
2.   Answers will vary.
3.
4.

Ask again: _____

Use the information above to write a paragraph. Ask the question. State the reasons, and then ask the question again. Indent the first sentence. Use capital letters and periods. Remember to give your paragraph a title.

Answers will vary.

57

Abbreviations

Write the correct abbreviation for each word on the line next to it.
Use a dictionary to check your answers for spelling and capitalization.

Street	St.	pound	lb.	minute	min.
Junior	Jr.	ounce	oz.	foot	ft.
Mister	Mr.	Senior	Sr.	inch	in.
Doctor	Dr.	centimeter	cm	President	Pres.
Apartment	Apt.	Road	Rd.	Mountain	Mt.

Subtraction Review

Subtract to solve each problem.

A.
| 623 − 194 = 429 | 900 − 309 = 591 | 722 − 317 = 405 | 377 − 186 = 191 | 871 − 384 = 487 | 628 − 300 = 328 |

| 990 − 731 = 259 | 818 − 693 = 125 | 572 − 335 = 237 | 951 − 357 = 594 | 825 − 469 = 356 | 771 − 217 = 554 |

Write the answers in order from smallest to largest.

125   191   237   259   328   356

405   429   487   554   591   594

58

Subtraction with Decimals

Subtract to solve each problem.

A.
| 20.20 − 13.75 = 6.45 | B. 334.5 − 145.6 = 188.9 | C. 7.051 − 2.058 = 4.993 |

D.
| 3.812 − 2.116 = 1.696 | E. 8.229 − 2.443 = 5.786 | F. 421.6 − 334.7 = 86.9 |

Contractions

Read each sentence. Circle the correct contraction for the highlighted words.

1. I did not look at the movie when it was scary! — (didn't) did'nt don't
2. You are my best friend! — You'd You'll (You're)
3. Are you sure we are on the right path? — we'd we'll (we're)
4. Brian said he is older than you. — he'd (he's) he'll
5. Who would want to live in that dusty old house? — (Who'd) Who's Who've
6. They are very kind people. — They'll (They're) They've
7. Let us begin the lesson. — Lets (Let's) Lets'
8. You are going to be late for school. — Your'e (You're) Your
9. You have given me plenty of reasons to study. — You'd You're (You've)
10. I am going to the zoo tomorrow. — I'd I'll (I'm)

59

Pronouns

Read each sentence. Replace the highlighted word(s) with the correct pronoun by writing it on the lines.

1. Jim and Carla like to ride motorcycles. __They__ ride whenever they can.
2. Jane has two lovebirds. __She__ sings to them every day.
3. Chelsea and Cheyna are sisters. Let's go to their house and play with __them__.
4. Billy is a police officer. __He__ likes to help people.
5. This book is from my grandparents. __It__ is my favorite.
6. Daphne and I like jelly beans. __We__ like to eat the red ones.
7. That is Rocky's baseball. Please give it to __him__.

Subtraction with Decimals

Subtract to solve each problem.

A.
| 8.5 − 2.8 = 5.7 | B. 9.2 − 7.5 = 1.7 | C. 7.1 − 4.1 = 3.0 |

D.
| 3.75 − 2.12 = 1.63 | E. 54.3 − 19.4 = 34.9 | F. 9.35 − 5.68 = 3.67 |

G.
| 2.01 − 1.95 = .06 | H. 5.12 − 4.08 = 1.04 | I. 53.0 − 22.6 = 30.4 |

If the answers were dollar amounts, which problem would you like? [E]

60

Building Vocabulary

Ike and Spike are two young boys. Read the story to find out some of the messes they get themselves involved in. Then, read each of the five sentences. Write the letter for the best answer on the line.

Ike, Spike, and the Circle Game

Ike and Spike are two brave little boys who will try anything once. There's just one problem. These eight-year-old friends can never agree. They always want to do things in different ways. That's quite a dilemma sometimes.

Once they created a large mural. Ike's faces were smiling, and Spike's faces all frowned. Another day, the boys went for a long hike. Ike took the path up into the hills, and Spike walked down by the river. They didn't find each other again until the next day.

Here you see them struggling to get home from a fishing excursion. Each boy wants to go a different way. These poor guys have been spinning in circles for an hour. Maybe soon one will get tired so they can at least move the boat!

B 1. The word dilemma means:
   a. canoe   b. problem   c. bait   d. song

A 2. the word created means:
   a. made   b. heard   c. told   d. found

C 3. The word struggling means:
   a. laughing   b. running   c. trying hard   d. painting

C 4. The word excursion means:
   a. hat   b. lesson   c. trip   d. fort

D 5. A word in the story that is a synonym for varied is:
   a. ordinary   b. poor   c. problem   d. different

Practice New Words

On a separate sheet of paper, write one sentence using each of these words.

dilemma   created   struggling   excursion

61

Mixed Problems with Decimals

Add or subtract to solve each problem.

A.
| 726.6 + 122.5 = 849.1 | B. 9.025 − 1.874 = 7.151 | C. 423.8 + 111.4 = 535.2 |

D.
| 8.345 + 2.137 = 10.482 | E. 77.61 − 44.32 = 33.29 | F. 522.7 + 311.7 = 834.4 |

List the answers from largest to smallest.

849.1
834.4
535.2
33.29
10.482
7.151

Using Guide Words

Look at the words in the word list. Print each word in alphabetical order below the two guide words it would appear between in a dictionary.

1. aardvark afghan	2. Africa aim
aboard	after
about	aggravate
above	agree
affect	aid
afford	ailment

Word List
aggravate
above
aboard
affect
about
after
aid
agree
ailment
afford

62

Understanding What I've Read

Parasites

Some animals get their food by living in or on other things. These animals, called parasites, do not kill the animals they live on, but they may harm or irritate them. A flea will live on a dog, cat, or other animals. The animal it lives on is called the host. The flea gets its food by sucking the other animal's blood. The flea will not harm the host, but it will make the host itch and feel uncomfortable. Some worms are also parasites. A tapeworm lives inside the body of an animal. It eats the food the host has eaten. The tapeworm can make the host very sick. Plants can be parasites, too. Mistletoe and some types of ferns live on trees, taking food and water from them.

1. What is the main idea of this story?
   a. Parasites live on or in other living things.
   b. A flea is a parasite.
   c. Parasites can make their hosts sick.

2. How does a flea get food?
   It sucks its host's blood.

3. Where does a tapeworm live?
   It lives inside the body of an animal.

4. What is a parasite?
   It is an animal that lives and feeds in or on other things.

5. What does the word host mean?
   a. an animal that lives on another living thing
   b. the animal a parasite lives on
   c. mistletoe

6. What kinds of plants can be parasites?
   Mistletoe and some ferns

63

Beat the Clock (Multiplication Facts 0 to 9)

A.
| 7 ×4 = 28 | 4 ×6 = 24 | 1 ×3 = 3 | 9 ×5 = 45 | 1 ×4 = 4 | 4 ×8 = 32 | 8 ×6 = 48 | 0 ×6 = 0 | 5 ×5 = 25 |

B.
| 8 ×1 = 8 | 4 ×0 = 0 | 3 ×3 = 9 | 4 ×3 = 12 | 3 ×5 = 15 | 9 ×2 = 18 | 3 ×7 = 21 | 8 ×9 = 72 | 7 ×2 = 14 |

C.
| 5 ×4 = 20 | 2 ×0 = 0 | 8 ×7 = 56 | 0 ×1 = 0 | 1 ×5 = 5 | 7 ×4 = 28 | 1 ×6 = 6 | 3 ×8 = 24 | 9 ×0 = 0 |

D.
| 7 ×1 = 7 | 4 ×9 = 36 | 6 ×7 = 42 | 9 ×0 = 0 | 0 ×7 = 0 | 9 ×5 = 45 | 6 ×7 = 42 | 1 ×3 = 3 | 4 ×3 = 12 |

E.
| 0 ×9 = 0 | 8 ×5 = 40 | 3 ×2 = 6 | 5 ×6 = 30 | 1 ×1 = 1 | 4 ×9 = 36 | 0 ×0 = 0 | 4 ×1 = 4 | 2 ×10 = 20 |

F.
| 7 ×7 = 49 | 3 ×9 = 27 | 1 ×5 = 5 | 0 ×1 = 0 | 6 ×6 = 36 | 4 ×1 = 4 | 2 ×6 = 12 | 4 ×6 = 24 | 2 ×5 = 10 |

G.
| 9 ×3 = 27 | 7 ×7 = 9 | 4 ×0 = 0 | 0 ×16 = 0 | 4 ×5 = 40 | 9 ×9 = 81 | 8 ×2 = 64 | 6 ×8 = 0 | 0 ×0 = 0 |

H.
| 2 ×8 = 16 | 6 ×4 = 24 | 6 ×9 = 54 | 1 ×7 = 7 | 7 ×5 = 35 | 8 ×4 = 32 | 0 ×0 = 0 | 9 ×8 = 72 | 3 ×7 = 21 | 9 ×7 = 63 |

I.
| 7 ×5 = 35 | 8 ×0 = 0 | 6 ×4 = 24 | 3 ×5 = 15 | 3 ×6 = 18 | 9 ×8 = 48 | 7 ×2 = 14 | 1 ×2 = 2 | 9 ×7 = 63 |

J.
| 8 ×2 = 16 | 9 ×2 = 18 | 0 ×7 = 0 | 7 ×8 = 56 | 2 ×5 = 10 | 9 ×2 = 18 | 6 ×9 = 54 | 1 ×8 = 8 | 6 ×5 = 30 |

Time: _____   Number correct: _____

64

151

Answer Key

Antonyms, Synonyms, and Homonyms — Language Arts

Use the clues below to solve the crossword puzzle.

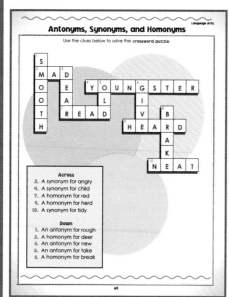

Crossword answers: SMOOTH, MAD, YOUNGSTER, SEAL, LIVE, READ, B, HEARD, REAL, BRAKE, NEAT

Across
2. A synonym for angry
4. A synonym for child
7. A homonym for red
9. A homonym for herd
10. A synonym for tidy

Down
1. An antonym for rough
3. A homonym for deer
5. An antonym for new
6. An antonym for take
8. A homonym for break

64

69

Multiplication Facts — Math

Fill in the numbers to complete the facts.

A.
8 × 3 = 24
10 × [9] = 63
11 × [3] = 30
11 × [3] = 33
8 × [8] = 64
3 × 6 = 18
10 × 7 = [70]

B.
12 × [2] = 24
10 × 8 = 80
[4] × 9 = 36
8 × 9 = [72]
10 × 9 = [90]
12 × 3 = 36
8 × 3 = 24

C.
12 × 9 = [108]
6 × [9] = 54
10 × [4] = 40
12 × 5 = [60]
10 × 2 = 20
[8] × 3 = 24
9 × [8] = 72

Writing Contractions — Grammar

Create as many contractions as you can by using the words below. Write the contractions on the lines at the bottom of the page. Number the words as you write them.

Word bank: are, can, not, could, do, have, he, here, is, I, it, will, she, should, would, there, they

he's, he'll, he'd, I've, aren't, I'll, I'd, can't, isn't, couldn't, she's, don't, she'll, haven't, she'd, shouldn't, there's, they're, they'll, they'd, won't, wouldn't

70

70

Prefixes — Language Arts

Use the prefix bank and word list to create as many words as you can. Write the words on the lines. Use another sheet of paper if needed.

Prefix Bank: dis- in- pre- re- un-

Word List: able, form, close, fill, civilized, miss, capable, come, wind, dent, charge, qualify, related, sole, pay, heat, cover, view

1. disable
2. disclose
3. dismiss
4. discharge
5. disqualify
6. discover
7. incapable
8. income
9. indent
10. inform
11. insole
12. preheat
13. prepay
14. preview
15. recover
16. refill
17. reform
18. repay
19. review
20. rewind — uncover
21. unable — unrelated
22. uncivilized — unwind

How Many? — Math

Multiply. Circle all the odd answers.

A.
11 × 6 = 66
7 × 8 = 56
10 × 6 = 60
12 × 6 = 72
(5 × 9 = 45)
9 × 4 = 36
12 × 5 = 60

B.
10 × 4 = 40
(9 × 3 = 27)
(11 × 7 = 77)
3 × 8 = 24
8 × 8 = 64
10 × 2 = 20
(7 × 9 = 63)

C.
11 × 2 = 22
10 × 9 = 90
2 × 9 = 18
5 × 8 = 40
(10 × 1 = 10)
(11 × 9 = 99)
10 × 7 = 70

71

Building Vocabulary — Reading Comprehension

Gordy the gorilla and Tussie the elephant are good friends. Read the story to learn more about one of their adventures. Then, read each of the five sentences. Write the letter for the best answer on the line.

Friends to the End

Tussie and Gordy are the best of friends. After all, they are the two largest and loudest creatures in the jungle. There was a time when they feared each other. Now they find that they can actually help each other. Sometimes Gordy will scrub Tussie's huge, gray back. Tussie returns the favor by making her trunk into a shower for Gordy.

Once they combined efforts to do something quite noble. A newborn tiger cub had wandered into the jungle. The cub's parents were worried and came to Gordy and Tussie for help. Tussie made big, wide paths through the thick jungle. Gordy swung from tree to tree looking everywhere. Together, in an hour's time, they found the tiger cub. Everyone was pleased!

1. The word **actually** means: **D**
   a. slowly   b. hotly   c. angrily   d. really
2. The word **favor** means: **B**
   a. drink   b. good deed   c. surprise   d. dark night
3. The word **combined** means: **C**
   a. pointed   b. slid   c. joined   d. yelled
4. The word **noble** means: **B**
   a. furry   b. good   c. calm   d. bad
5. A word in the story that is a synonym for searching is: **C**
   a. scrubbing   b. worried   c. looking   d. pleasing

Practice New Words

On a separate sheet of paper, write one sentence using each of these words:

actually   favor   combined   noble

72

72

Find the Missing Factors — Math

Write the missing factor to complete each fact.

A.
4 × [3] = 12
[0] × 5 = 0
8 × [5] = 40

B.
[8] × 3 = 24
3 × [9] = 27
[7] × 9 = 63

C.
5 × [7] = 35
[18] × 1 = 18
9 × [2] = 18

D.
6 × [6] = 36
[5] × 6 = 30
[5] × 9 = 45

Homonyms — Language Arts

Read each sentence below. Circle the homonym that completes each sentence correctly.

1. While in the woods, Kristen saw a (**bear** / bare).
2. Candy fell and hurt her (**toe** / tow).
3. The (sale / **sail**) on the boat billowed in the wind.
4. Sherry did not feel well and looked (pail / **pale**).
5. Teddy does not (**know** / no) how to play basketball.
6. We went to the mailbox and (cent / **sent**) a letter.
7. My cat had six kittens and four of them are (mail / **male**).
8. Sissy stopped to pick a (flour / **flower**) from the garden.

73

73

Multiplication Word Problems — Math

Use multiplication to solve each word problem.

A. Stephen, Wendy, and Spencer each spent $9 at the amusement park. How much money did they spend altogether? $ **27**

B. Jennifer likes to make dolls. If she makes 3 dolls each day for 6 days, how many dolls will she have made? **18** dolls

C. Tory keeps his race cars in shoe boxes. He has 11 boxes with 5 cars in each. How many race cars does Tory have? **55** race cars

D. Tamika rode her bike for 2 hours every day for 8 days. How many hours did she ride altogether in those 8 days? **16** hours

E. Justin, Dylan, and Stephanie all wear hats. If they each have 12 hats, how many hats do they have altogether? **36** hats

F. Ursula had 3 mother cats. Each mother cat had 5 kittens. How many kittens did Ursula's cats have altogether? **15** kittens

G. Sean collects postage stamps. He puts 12 stamps on each page of his album. If Sean has 8 filled pages, how many stamps does Sean have? **96** stamps

H. Denise built 7 towers with building blocks. If she used 8 blocks for each tower, how many blocks did she use in all? **56** blocks

I. Gina wants to make friendship necklaces. She will use 9 beads on each necklace. How many beads does Gina need to make 5 necklaces? **45** beads

74

Compare and Contrast — Writing

Fill in the blanks to compare and contrast a newspaper and a book. The first one has been done for you.

Newspaper — contrast — compare — Book — contrast

(Venn diagram: large pages / two stories / small pages)

Write two paragraphs below. In the first paragraph, tell how newspapers and books are alike. Tell how each is different in the second paragraph. Be sure to indent the first sentence of each paragraph.

Answers will vary.

75

Match the Fact to the Answer — Math

4 × 5 = | 8
2 × 7 = | 18
8 × 1 = | 3
9 × 2 = | 15
5 × 3 = | 14

1 × 5 = | 24
5 × 3 = | 15
3 × 8 = | 24
2 × 6 = | 12
7 × 3 = | 15

6 × 3 = | 40
0 × 9 = | 6
1 × 7 = | 8
8 × 5 = | 40
6 × 1 = | 6

Proper Nouns — Grammar

Underline each proper noun in the story below. Write the correct capital letter above each proper noun. The first one has been done for you.

C   M   D B I   I   A M U
Last christmas mom, dad, billy, isabel, and I went to aunt mable and uncle

B   K   T
buddy's house. All of our relatives were there having a good time. keisha, taylor,

M   S   C   A   K
and maya all got new sneakers from santa claus. alex and kelli brought a pie for

M   D   D   U
mrs. davis. The twins, dustin and dillon, showed off their new baby sister, stephanie.

J
jamie brought her new doll. Everyone had a good time and looks forward to getting

N Y D
together on new year's day.

76

Understanding What I've Read — Reading Comprehension

Space Probes

We learn about planets by observing, or studying, them. Scientists use telescopes to see planets. A telescope is a special instrument that makes faraway objects look bigger. Some planets are too far away to see clearly, even when we use a telescope. How can we learn about these planets? Scientists send special spacecraft called probes into space. Telescopes and cameras are sent in the probe to record everything they see. Probes also carry special instruments to examine the weather and soil on other planets. The information is sent back to Earth where scientists can study it. The first probe, called Mariner 2, was launched in 1962. It gave us information about the planet Venus. Since then, scientists have sent over 25 probes into space. Each probe tells us even more about other planets.

1. What is the main idea of this story?
   a. Probes tell us about other planets.
   b. Telescopes help us to see other planets.
   c. Mariner 2 was the first space probe.

2. What is a probe?
   a spacecraft sent to investigate

3. What information about other planets can a probe gather?
   weather, type of soil, what it looks like

4. What does the word **observe** mean?
   a. a special instrument
   b. to study
   c. probe

5. What special equipment do probes carry?
   telescopes and cameras

77

152

Answer Key

A Multiplication Puzzle

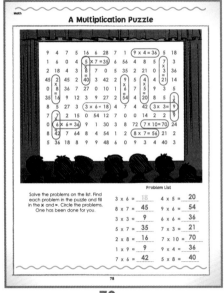

Problem List

Solve the problems on the list. Find each problem in the puzzle and fill in the x and =. Circle the problems. One has been done for you.

3 x 6 = 18	4 x 5 = 20
8 x 7 = 45	9 x 6 = 54
3 x 3 = 9	6 x 6 = 36
5 x 7 = 35	7 x 3 = 21
2 x 8 = 16	7 x 10 = 70
1 x 9 = 9	9 x 4 = 36
7 x 6 = 42	5 x 8 = 40

78

Descriptive Writing

The three adjectives below describe the picture. Add two more adjectives of your own. Write a paragraph about the picture using these adjectives. Remember to indent the first sentence of your paragraph and to include a title.

1. cheesy   2. messy   3. spicy
4. _____

Answers will vary.

Basic Facts

A.	B.	C.
0 x 4 = 0	2 x 5 = 10	8 x 0 = 0
1 x 9 = 9	6 x 6 = 36	4 x 10 = 40
5 x 7 = 35	0 x 7 = 0	2 x 1 = 2
3 x 4 = 12	1 x 3 = 3	8 x 8 = 64
2 x 9 = 18	8 x 11 = 88	9 x 6 = 54
7 x 6 = 42	6 x 8 = 48	5 x 6 = 30

Bonus: Circle the even answers. Draw a square around the odd number answers.

79

One-Digit Times Two-Digit Multiplication

Multiply to solve the problems.

A.
21 x 9 = 189	70 x 0 = 0	42 x 3 = 126	76 x 6 = 456

B.
98 x 1 = 98	61 x 2 = 122	21 x 4 = 84	22 x 2 = 44

C.
64 x 4 = 256	29 x 5 = 145	38 x 7 = 266	56 x 9 = 504

Punctuation Review

Add the correct **punctuation** at the end of each sentence.

1. Who won the big football game **?**
2. I went to the zoo last week with Tony **.**
3. Please pass the salt **.**
4. I would like to learn to sew **.**
5. I cannot believe he did that **!**
6. I can't get out of this tree. Help **!**
7. Katie used to live in Texas **.**
8. That ladder is going to fall. Look out **!**
9. We are going to the lake **.**
10. When is Elliott's birthday **?**

80

Sequencing Events

Read the story to learn about the old house. Then, read the sentences below. Decide what happened first, second, and so on. Number the sentences in the correct order.

The Old House

Jerome was the one who discovered the old house in the first place. It was late one day last October. Jerome had taken a shortcut through the woods and there it was! That house was so spooky, it scared him just to look at it.

The next day at school, Jerome told Lisa Peterson. By the time the school day was through, the whole school knew about the house. All of the kids wanted to see it. A group of Jerome's friends planned to meet there right after dinner.

Nearly 20 boys and girls showed up at the house just before 6 o'clock. They walked around the old empty building in a close group.

Suddenly, they all heard a loud shriek. Everyone jumped and some children even screamed. Jerome looked up at one of the window ledges. There sat a big, black crow. All of the children laughed. They had let their imaginations get the best of them. They knew then that the house was not really scary. They all agreed that it had been a fun-filled adventure just the same.

5 The children walked around the house.
2 Jerome told Lisa Peterson about the house.
7 The children knew the house was not scary.
1 Jerome discovered the old house.
6 The children saw a crow on a ledge.
4 Nearly 20 boys and girls showed up at the old house before 6 o'clock.
3 Some of Jerome's friends planned to meet at the old house after dinner.

81

One-Digit Times Three-Digit Multiplication

Multiply to solve the problems.

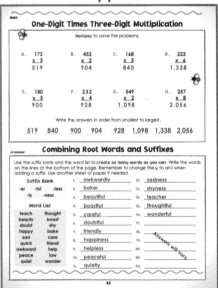

A. 173 x 3 = 519	B. 452 x 2 = 904	C. 168 x 5 = 840	D. 223 x 6 = 1,338
E. 180 x 5 = 900	F. 232 x 4 = 928	G. 549 x 2 = 1,098	H. 257 x 8 = 2,056

Write the answers in order from smallest to largest.

519 840 900 904 928 1,098 1,338 2,056

Combining Root Words and Suffixes

Use the suffix bank and the word list to **create as many words as you can**. Write the words on the lines at the bottom of the page. Remember to change the y to an i when adding a suffix. Use another sheet of paper if needed.

Suffix Bank
-er   -ful   -less
-ly   -ness

Word List
teach   thought
beauty   boast
doubt   shy
happy   bake
sad   care
quick   friend
awkward   help
peace   law
quiet   wonder

1. awkwardly
2. baker
3. beautiful
4. boastful
5. careful
6. doubtful
7. friendly
8. happiness
9. helpless
10. peaceful
11. quietly
12. sadness
13. shyness
14. teacher
15. thoughtful
16. wonderful
17. _____
18. _____
19. _____
20. _____

Answers will vary.

82

Compound Words

Fill in each blank with a word from the word list to make a **compound word**. Use each word only once.

Word List   boat   shore   case   fly   nap   bug
board   burger   crow   coat   book   time

scare crow	night time
cook book	cheese burger
cat nap	sea shore
steam boat	horse fly
suit case	chalk board
rain coat	lady bug

Story Problems

Solve each word problem.

A. The Super Coaster roller coaster ride has 15 cars. Each car has 4 seats. How many people can ride the Super Coaster at one time?
60 people

B. Last week, 21 mother dogs had puppies. If they each had 6 puppies, how many puppies did the dogs have altogether?   126 puppies

C. Cheri can make 32 bracelets a week. She made bracelets for 12 weeks. How many bracelets did Cheri make?   384 bracelets

D. Sixteen packages of crayons were donated to Mr. Horowitz's class. Each package had 64 crayons. How many crayons were donated in all?
1,024 crayons

83

Greater Than or Less Than?

Multiply to solve the problems. Write **>** or **<** in the box to show if the first answer is greater or less than the second answer.

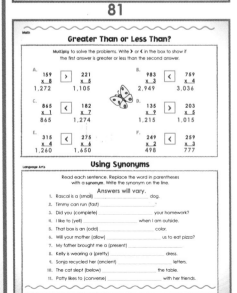

A. 159 x 8 = 1,272 **>** 221 x 5 = 1,105	B. 983 x 3 = 2,949 **<** 759 x 4 = 3,036
C. 865 x 1 = 865 **<** 182 x 7 = 1,274	D. 135 x 9 = 1,215 **>** 203 x 5 = 1,015
E. 315 x 4 = 1,260 **<** 275 x 6 = 1,650	F. 249 x 2 = 498 **<** 259 x 3 = 777

Using Synonyms

Read each sentence. Replace the word in parentheses with a **synonym**. Write the synonym on the line.

Answers will vary.

1. Rascal is a (small) _____ dog.
2. Timmy can run (fast) _____
3. Did you (complete) _____ your homework?
4. I like to (yell) _____ when I am outside.
5. That box is an (odd) _____ color.
6. Will your mother (allow) _____ us to eat pizza?
7. My father brought me a (present) _____
8. Kelly is wearing a (pretty) _____ dress.
9. Sonja recycled her (ancient) _____ letters.
10. The cat slept (below) _____ the table.
11. Patty likes to (converse) _____ with her friends.

84

Synonym Search

Match each pair of synonyms in the box below by connecting a word from the first column to a word in the second column. Then, find and circle each synonym pair in the word search. (Hint: Each pair of words is spelled across or down and does not share any letters.)

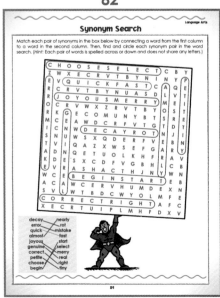

decay — rot
error — mistake
quick — fast
almost — nearly
joyous — merry
genuine — real
correct — right
petite — tiny
choose — select
begin — start

89

Interpreting a Grid

The children in Mr. Price's class made a **grid** showing the pets they own. Each check mark stands for one pet owned by a child. Use the grid to answer the questions.

Pets Owned by Mr. Price's Students

	Keisha	Juan	Maria	Tim	Anthony
turtle		✓	✓		✓
rabbit	✓	✓			
snake	✓				
lizard			✓	✓	
mouse	✓	✓			
fish		✓	✓	✓	
cat	✓	✓	✓	✓	✓
dog	✓	✓		✓	

A. What is the total number of pets listed on the grid?   21
B. Which child owns the most pets?   Juan
C. Which type of pet is owned by every child?   cat
D. How many children own turtles?   2
E. How many more pets does Maria have than Tim?   1
F. Does Anthony have a pet turtle?   yes   a rabbit?   no
G. What pets does Juan not own?   snake, lizard

90

153

Answer Key

Finish the Sentences

Read each sentence. Using the word list below, fill in each blank with a word that means the same as the highlighted word in each sentence.

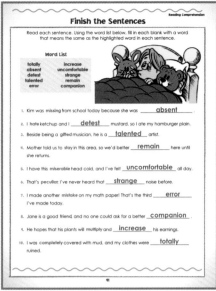

Word List

totally
absent
detest
talented
error
increase
uncomfortable
strange
remain
companion

1. Kim was missing from school today because she was __absent__.
2. I hate ketchup and I __detest__ mustard, so I ate my hamburger plain.
3. Beside being a gifted musician, he is a __talented__ artist.
4. Mother told us to stay in this area, so we'd better __remain__ here until she returns.
5. I have this miserable head cold, and I've felt __uncomfortable__ all day.
6. That's peculiar, I've never heard that __strange__ noise before.
7. I made another mistake on my math paper! That's the third __error__ I've made today.
8. Jane is a good friend, and no one could ask for a better __companion__.
9. He hopes that his plants will multiply and __increase__ his earnings.
10. I was completely covered with mud, and my clothes were __totally__ ruined.

91

Show Your Work

Multiply to solve each problem.

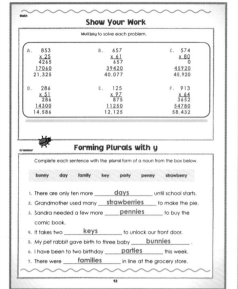

A. 853
× 25
4265
17060
21,325

B. 657
× 61
657
39420
40,077

C. 574
× 80
0
45920
45,920

D. 286
× 51
286
14300
14,586

E. 125
× 97
875
11250
12,125

F. 913
× 64
3652
54780
58,432

Forming Plurals with y

Complete each sentence with the plural form of a noun from the box below.

bunny   day   family   key   party   penny   strawberry

1. There are only ten more __days__ until school starts.
2. Grandmother used many __strawberries__ to make the pie.
3. Sandra needed a few more __pennies__ to buy the comic book.
4. It takes two __keys__ to unlock our front door.
5. My pet rabbit gave birth to three baby __bunnies__.
6. I have been to two birthday __parties__ this week.
7. There were __families__ in line at the grocery store.

92

Forming Plurals with f

Rewrite each word in the box as a plural on the line.

1. I would like to buy three __loaves__ of bread.
2. Place the encyclopedias on those __shelves__.
3. The __calves__ stood close to their mothers.
4. The __wolves__ were hunting for food.
5. We wore our __scarves__ outside in the snow.
6. A whole is made up of two __halves__.

loaf
shelf
calf
wolf
scarf
half

Show Your Work Again

Multiply to solve each problem.

525
× 51
525
26250
26,775

917
× 22
1834
18340
20,174

816
× 87
5712
57280
70,992

950
× 16
5700
9500
15,200

835
× 10
0
8350
8,350

727
× 31
727
21810
22,537

93

What's Wrong?

Read each paragraph. Underline the sentence in each paragraph that does not belong. The first one has been done for you.

1. Martha's dad is an electrician. He does many different kinds of things when he goes to work. Some days he checks the wiring in peoples' homes. Sometimes he checks the wiring in large buildings and shopping centers. Martha is very proud of him. He often helps put all the electrical wires and outlets in new buildings.

2. Jeremy has many reasons for wanting to be a dentist. He thinks having healthy teeth is very important. He has always been interested in all the things his own dentist does. Jeremy thinks he would be a good dentist, too. He has always enjoyed school.

3. Being a florist takes special training. You must know the names of all the flowers and plants. People who are in the hospital like to receive flowers. You must learn how to care for flowers and plants. It is also important to know how to arrange them.

4. Carl wants to be a teacher, but he can't decide what to teach. At first, he thought he would like to teach math. Then, he thought he would like to teach kindergarten. Carl likes many things. Now he thinks he would like to teach history.

How Much Money?

Calculate the money in each piggy bank and print the total on the line. Use a dollar sign and a decimal point for each amount.

A. 2 dimes, 4 pennies, 5 quarters — $1.49
B. 5 nickels, 6 dimes, 2 quarters — $1.35

C. 8 quarters, 2 dimes, 68 pennies — $2.88
D. 5 pennies, 12 dimes, 10 nickels — $1.75

94

Contraction Fun

Rewrite the words below as contractions. Use the key to create a patchwork design pattern at the bottom of the page.

1. she will __she'll__
2. you are __you're__
3. he would __he'd__
4. there is __there's__
5. I am __I'm__
6. can not __can't__
7. they are __they're__
8. should not __shouldn't__
9. what is __what's__
10. they will __they'll__
11. we would __we'd__
12. we are __we're__

If the word ends in	Draw this pattern in the grid
'll	
're	
'd	
's	
'm	
t	

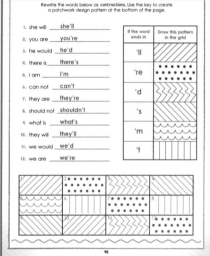

95

Solve the Code

Multiply and solve the code to find out who wins the race. Use a calculator.

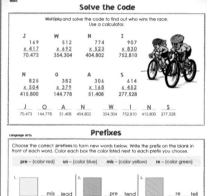

J 169 × 417 = 70,473
W 512 × 692 = 354,304
N 774 × 523 = 404,802
I 907 × 830 = 752,810

N 825 × 504 = 415,800
O 382 × 379 = 144,778
A 306 × 168 = 51,408
S 614 × 452 = 277,528

J O A N   W I N S
70,473 144,778 51,408 404,802   354,304 752,810 415,800 277,528

Prefixes

Choose the correct prefixes to form new words below. Write the prefix on the blank in front of each word. Color each box the color listed next to each prefix you choose.

pre – (color red)   un – (color blue)   mis – (color yellow)   re – (color green)

1. __mis__ lead
2. __pre__ tend
3. __re__ tell
4. __pre__ fix
5. __un__ fair
6. __un__ happy
7. __re__ flex
8. __mis__ conduct
9. __re__ fill

96

Analogies

Compare the relationships of the words below. Find the missing word for each analogy and write it in the space provided.

1. in : out :: up : __down__
2. two : four :: three : __six__
3. snow : cold :: sun : __warm__
4. mother : aunt :: father : __uncle__
5. ear : hear :: eye : __see__
6. she : her :: he : __him__
7. dog : bark :: bird : __chirp__
8. brother : boy :: sister : __girl__
9. bear : den :: bee : __hive__
10. finger : hand :: toe : __foot__
11. girl : mother :: boy : __father__
12. left : right :: top : __bottom__

Learning to Divide

Divide to solve each problem.

A. 4⟌32 = 8
B. 2⟌10 = 5
C. 5⟌45 = 9
D. 2⟌18 = 9
E. 7⟌35 = 5
F. 6⟌54 = 9
G. 2⟌12 = 6
H. 3⟌36 = 12

97

Division Designs

Divide. Then connect the dots in order, beginning with the number given first.

Start at 5.
A. 45 ÷ 9 = 5
B. 12 ÷ 2 = 6
C. 36 ÷ 6 = 6
D. 6 ÷ 3 = 2
E. 8 ÷ 8 = 1
F. 35 ÷ 5 = 7
G. 7 ÷ 7 = 1
H. 24 ÷ 4 = 6
I. 42 ÷ 6 = 7
J. 6 ÷ 2 = 3
K. 27 ÷ 9 = 3
L. 2 ÷ 1 = 2
M. 54 ÷ 9 = 6

Start at 6.
A. 18 ÷ 3 = 6
B. 20 ÷ 4 = 5
C. 10 ÷ 5 = 2
D. 24 ÷ 6 = 4
E. 14 ÷ 7 = 2
F. 64 ÷ 8 = 8
G. 5 ÷ 5 = 1
H. 48 ÷ 6 = 8
I. 49 ÷ 7 = 7
J. 42 ÷ 7 = 6
K. 2 ÷ 2 = 1

Linking Verbs

A linking verb does not show action but shows a state of being. It connects the subject of a sentence to a word or phrase that describes or renames the subject. Linking verbs include forms of to be, such as am, is, are, was, and were.

Example: The cow was black and white.

Read each sentence. Circle the linking verb.

1. Mary (was) happy when so many people attended her dance recital.
2. Kelsey (is) sorry she missed the party.
3. Mysteries (are) my favorite type of book!
4. Today (is) January third.
5. We (were) pleased to see our team win the game.
6. Kay (was) amused when Ken told jokes.
7. I (am) anxious to finish my homework before dinner.
8. Mr. Alton (was) quiet during the concert.

98

Identifying Parts of Speech

Read each sentence. Decide if the highlighted word is an adjective, an adverb, a noun, or a verb. Use the key to write Adj, Adv, N, or V, on the line.

Key			
Adj – adjective	Adv – adverb	N – noun	V – verb

1. __Adj__ The big, red apple fell off the tree.
2. __N__ The yellow dog followed Trina.
3. __V__ Sarah fell down the stairs.
4. __N__ Broccoli is on sale at the market today.
5. __Adv__ Kenny slowly walked to school.
6. __Adj__ My new sweater is very warm.
7. __V__ Mariah sprinted across the meadow.
8. __Adj__ The winner of the race cried tears of joy.
9. __N__ The tornado did not damage any homes.

Story Problems

Solve the story problems.

A. Patricia bought 16 doughnuts for herself and her 3 friends. If they each eat the same number of doughnuts, how many will each person eat? __4__

B. Catherine has 7 days to knit 21 sweaters. If she knits the same number of sweaters each day, how many will she have to make each day? __3__

C. Victoria picked 72 apples and used them to make pies. She used 6 apples in each pie. How many pies did Victoria make? __12__

99

Answer Key

100 — Descriptive Writing

Read the short paragraph.

It was a nice day. Without warning, a storm suddenly blew in over the lake. We were afraid our boat would sink.

Here are some adjectives that can help describe the sentences:

What kind of day it was: bright, sunny, lovely, warm, spring
How the storm came in: quickly, gusting, swirling, howling, thundering, booming
What the storm looked like: dark, cloudy, windy, blackness, inky
What the people looked like: pale, tense, worried, frightened

Rewrite the paragraph to make it more colorful and interesting. Use the adjectives above or think of your own to describe what has happened in the paragraph. Give the paragraph a title.

Paragraphs will vary.

101 — Beat the Clock (Division Facts 1 to 4)

A.	36 ÷ 6 = 6	8 ÷ 1 = 8	45 ÷ 9 = 5	16 ÷ 8 = 2	35 ÷ 5 = 7
B.	24 ÷ 8 = 3	27 ÷ 9 = 3	20 ÷ 5 = 4	21 ÷ 3 = 7	12 ÷ 2 = 6
C.	20 ÷ 4 = 5	42 ÷ 7 = 6	18 ÷ 6 = 3	14 ÷ 2 = 7	28 ÷ 7 = 4
D.	56 ÷ 8 = 7	9 ÷ 3 = 3	3 ÷ 1 = 3	40 ÷ 8 = 5	12 ÷ 4 = 3
E.	10 ÷ 2 = 5	48 ÷ 6 = 8	45 ÷ 5 = 9	0 ÷ 6 = 0	15 ÷ 3 = 5
F.	7 ÷ 7 = 1	6 ÷ 2 = 3	18 ÷ 9 = 2	7 ÷ 1 = 7	32 ÷ 4 = 8
G.	5 ÷ 1 = 5	35 ÷ 5 = 7	56 ÷ 7 = 8	5 ÷ 5 = 0	30 ÷ 3 = 10
H.	18 ÷ 6 = 3	15 ÷ 5 = 3	18 ÷ 2 = 9	72 ÷ 8 = 9	2 ÷ 1 = 2
I.	30 ÷ 5 = 6	1 ÷ 1 = 1	21 ÷ 7 = 3	8 ÷ 4 = 2	0 ÷ 3 = 0
J.	9 ÷ 9 = 1	28 ÷ 4 = 7	16 ÷ 4 = 4	12 ÷ 2 = 6	36 ÷ 9 = 4
K.	8 ÷ 8 = 1	27 ÷ 9 = 3	6 ÷ 6 = 1	6 ÷ 3 = 2	0 ÷ 4 = 0
L.	12 ÷ 3 = 4	81 ÷ 9 = 9	0 ÷ 2 = 0	49 ÷ 7 = 7	36 ÷ 9 = 4
M.	30 ÷ 6 = 5	32 ÷ 8 = 4	9 ÷ 1 = 9	0 ÷ 8 = 0	14 ÷ 7 = 2
N.	35 ÷ 7 = 5	16 ÷ 2 = 8	0 ÷ 7 = 0	42 ÷ 6 = 7	6 ÷ 1 = 6
O.	45 ÷ 9 = 5	24 ÷ 4 = 6	10 ÷ 5 = 2	0 ÷ 1 = 0	12 ÷ 6 = 2
P.	2 ÷ 2 = 1	0 ÷ 5 = 0	24 ÷ 6 = 4	48 ÷ 8 = 6	4 ÷ 4 = 1
Q.	54 ÷ 6 = 9	27 ÷ 9 = 3	18 ÷ 3 = 6	25 ÷ 5 = 5	63 ÷ 9 = 7
R.	64 ÷ 8 = 8	4 ÷ 1 = 4	4 ÷ 4 = 1	0 ÷ 9 = 0	4 ÷ 2 = 2
S.	72 ÷ 8 = 9	63 ÷ 7 = 9	48 ÷ 8 = 6	27 ÷ 9 = 3	24 ÷ 8 = 3
T.	36 ÷ 9 = 4	54 ÷ 9 = 6	3 ÷ 3 = 1	40 ÷ 5 = 8	14 ÷ 7 = 2

Time: ___   Number correct: ___

102 — Sentences & Fragments

Read each group of words. If the group is only a fragment, write F on the line. If it is a sentence, write S on the line and add the correct ending punctuation. The first one has been done for you.

- S 1. Isabelle is a good dancer.
- F 2. To the park
- F 3. Ride in the car
- S 4. Be careful !
- S 5. Stacey liked the movie.
- S 6. Will you come over tomorrow ?
- F 7. On top of the house by the chimne
- F 8. With Tina and Gina

Division Designs

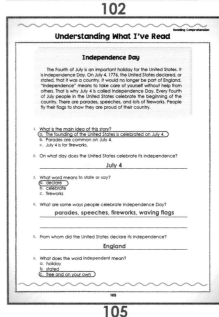

Divide. Then connect the dots in order, beginning with the number given first.

Start at 6
A. 30 ÷ 6 = 5   F. 56 ÷ 7 = 8
B. 15 ÷ 3 = 5   G. 6 ÷ 6 = 1
C. 28 ÷ 7 = 4   H. 21 ÷ 3 = 7
D. 20 ÷ 5 = 4   I. 40 ÷ 8 = 5
E. 9 ÷ 1 = 9   J. 48 ÷ 6 = 8

Start at 2
A. 5 ÷ 1 = 5   G. 45 ÷ 5 = 9
B. 63 ÷ 7 = 9   H. 12 ÷ 3 = 4
C. 9 ÷ 3 = 3   I. 21 ÷ 7 = 3
D. 8 ÷ 2 = 4   J. 63 ÷ 9 = 7
E. 18 ÷ 6 = 3   K. 25 ÷ 5 = 5
F. 56 ÷ 8 = 7

103 — Complete Subjects

Draw a line under the complete subject of each sentence below.

1. Astronauts are very brave people.
2. Donna's birthday is today.
3. The big, red boat sped across the water.
4. The spectators enjoyed the fireworks.
5. Barbara and Cindy love to garden.
6. The blue engine stopped at the station.
7. The actor was excellent in the play.
8. The movie was the best one I have ever seen!
9. Good health is important to everyone.
10. All children love to play.
11. The pictures in that book are beautiful.
12. The raft floated across the lake.

>, =, or <

Divide to solve each problem. Write >, =, or < to compare the answers.

A. 5)25 = 5   B. 7)35 = 5   A < F
C. 3)27 = 9   D. 4)32 = 8   D > B
E. 8)56 = 7   F. 7)49 = 7   C = G
G. 2)18 = 9   H. 9)36 = 4   E > H

104 — Division Practice

Divide to solve each problem.

A. 4)24 = 6   A. 9)72 = 8   C. 4)36 = 9   D. 7)70 = 10

E. 2)12 = 6   F. 4)16 = 4

G. 2)20 = 10   H. 3)21 = 7

Conjunctions

Select the correct conjunction to complete each sentence. Write it on the line.

and   but   or

1. I have enough money to buy both a ball __and__ a bat.
2. You may have either milk __or__ juice to drink.
3. Her favorite sandwich is peanut butter __and__ jelly.
4. John took swimming lessons, __but__ he still could not swim.
5. Mom said I can choose either pancakes __or__ waffles.
6. We will go either to the mountains __or__ the ocean on our vacation.
7. The United States' flag is red, white, __and__ blue.
8. Johnny worked very hard on his report, __but__ he only made a B.

105 — Understanding What I've Read

Independence Day

The Fourth of July is an important holiday for the United States. It is Independence Day. On July 4, 1776, the United States declared, or stated, that it was a country. It would no longer be part of England. "Independence" means to take care of yourself without help from others. That is why July 4 is called Independence Day. Every Fourth of July people in the United States celebrate the beginning of the country. There are parades, speeches, and lots of fireworks. People fly their flags to show they are proud of their country.

1. What is the main idea of this story?
   a. The founding of the United States is celebrated on July 4. ✓
   b. Parades are common on July 4.
   c. July 4 is for fireworks.

2. On what day does the United States celebrate its independence?
   July 4

3. What word means to state or say?
   a. declare ✓
   b. celebrate
   c. fireworks

4. What are some ways people celebrate Independence Day?
   parades, speeches, fireworks, waving flags

5. From whom did the United States declare its independence?
   England

6. What does the word independent mean?
   a. holiday
   b. stated
   c. free and on your own ✓

106 — Division

Divide to solve each problem.

A. 56 ÷ 7 = 8   B. 24 ÷ 8 = 3   C. 54 ÷ 9 = 6
D. 32 ÷ 8 = 4   E. 12 ÷ 3 = 4   F. 25 ÷ 5 = 5
G. 50 ÷ 5 = 10   H. 42 ÷ 7 = 6   I. 72 ÷ 9 = 8
J. 66 ÷ 6 = 11   K. 40 ÷ 5 = 8   L. 21 ÷ 3 = 7

Main Idea

The main idea of a paragraph is its central thought or topic. Read each paragraph and the three phrases below it. Decide which one tells the main idea. Write the letter of that phrase on the line.

a   Taffy's little brother was missing again. At least, no one knew where he was. Little Jeff could get into the strangest places. He would stay hidden until everyone got worried or mad. His favorite place to hide was in the clothes hamper. Taffy's mother said they should put a bell on Jeff!
   a. A mischievous boy   b. The clothes hamper   c. Taffy's family

b   Waterskiing is a lot of fun once you learn how. Sailing and boating are nice ways to spend a summer day. Water polo is fun to play. If you are near the ocean, bodysurfing and windsurfing are really exciting.
   a. Summertime   b. Water sports   c. Waterskiing

c   Ted asked his dad if he could have an allowance. Ted's dad said that he certainly could! He also said that Ted would have to do a few chores around the house. That was how he would earn his allowance. Every week Ted had to mow the lawn. He also had to take out the garbage. Ted had only been earning an allowance for three weeks. He was already thinking of asking for a raise!
   a. Cleaning the garage   b. Ted and his dad   c. Earning an allowance

107 — Writing Sentences

Read each pair of sentences. Rewrite the facts in a single sentence on the line.

1. Anna went to the beach. Anna wore her new bathing suit.
   Sentences will vary.
2. Billy hit a home run. Billy's team voted him the player of the game.
3. Charlie fell down the steps. Charlie was embarrassed.
4. Dianne went to the mall. Dianne bought a pair of jeans.
5. Eric painted a picture. Eric got paint on the floor.
6. Fran went to Gina's house. Fran and Gina played games.

Division Facts

Divide to solve each problem.

A. 63 ÷ 9 = 7   B. 49 ÷ 7 = 7   C. 15 ÷ 3 = 5
D. 64 ÷ 8 = 8   E. 30 ÷ 6 = 5   F. 80 ÷ 8 = 10
G. 12 ÷ 2 = 6   H. 45 ÷ 5 = 9   I. 81 ÷ 9 = 9

108 — Magic Trail

Follow the trail by solving the math problems. Can you find the magic number?

155

Answer Key

Division with Remainders

Divide to solve each problem.

A. $7\overline{)52}$ = 7 R3   B. $9\overline{)83}$ = 9 R2   C. $6\overline{)40}$ = 6 R4   D. $5\overline{)29}$ = 5 R4

E. $9\overline{)42}$ = 4 R6   F. $3\overline{)55}$ = 18 R1   G. $5\overline{)27}$ = 5 R2   H. $2\overline{)37}$ = 18 R1

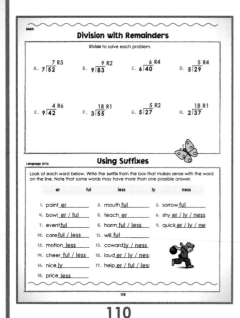

Using Suffixes

Look at each word below. Write the suffix from the box that makes sense with the word on the line. Note that some words may have more than one possible answer.

| er | ful | less | ly | ness |

1. paint **er**
2. mouth **ful**
3. sorrow **ful**
4. bowl **er / ful**
5. teach **er**
6. shy **er / ly / ness**
7. event **ful**
8. harm **ful / less**
9. quick **er / ly / ne**
10. care **ful / less**
11. will **ful**
12. motion **less**
13. coward **ly / ness**
14. cheer **ful / less**
15. loud **er / ly / ness**
16. nice **ly**
17. help **er / ful / less**
18. price **less**

110

Word Box Stories

Write eight words about the picture in the word box. Use the words to write a story. Be sure to use adjectives, capital letters, and periods. Give your story a title.

Things to Think About

Who is this story about?   Where does this story take place?
How does this story begin?   What happens next?
How will this story end?

Word Box

Stories will vary.

111

Root Words

Look at each word below. Write each root word on the line.

1. nonsense — sense
2. rewrite — write
3. spoonful — spoon
4. happiness — happy
5. kindness — kind
6. brotherhood — brother
7. ticklish — tickle
8. quickly — quick
9. baker — bake
10. lovable — love
11. helpless — help
12. cleanness — clean

Three-Digit Dividends

Divide to solve each problem.

A. $5\overline{)125}$ = 25   B. $6\overline{)468}$ = 78   C. $4\overline{)632}$ = 158   D. $9\overline{)945}$ = 105

E. $8\overline{)704}$ = 88   F. $2\overline{)778}$ = 389   G. $7\overline{)672}$ = 96   H. $7\overline{)784}$ = 112

112

Predicates

The simple predicate is a verb that tells what the subject did or what was done to the subject. The complete predicate includes the verb and all the words that tell more about it.

Example: The white cat slept on the pillow.

The simple predicate is slept and the complete predicate is slept on the pillow.

Underline the complete predicate of each sentence. Circle the simple predicate.

1. Bess danced in the school play.
2. We went to the mall after the library.
3. California is a state on the West Coast.
4. The weather began to turn cool.
5. It rained for hours yesterday!
6. Opal made a painting for her mom.
7. Snow fell for six hours.
8. Seven students were in the spelling bee.
9. The tractor made a loud noise.
10. We served ice cream and cake at the party.

Word Problems with Division

Read the word problems below. Solve each problem.

A. Jim, Steve, and Earl chartered a fishing boat. The trip cost $36. The men divided the cost of the trip between them equally. How much did each man have to pay?   **$ 12**

B. Jen has 21 dolls. If she puts the same number of dolls in 3 different doll houses, how many dolls will she put in each house?   **7 dolls**

C. Mabel had a dinner party for her friends. She prpared 24 meals and set up 4 tables. She wanted the same number of people at each table. How many people did she put at each table?   **6 people**

113

Main Idea

Circle or write the main idea of each paragraph.

1. It is September. It is the night of the first football game of the year. Everyone at Kidwell School is excited. Most excited of all is Cliff. This is the very first night he has ever marched with the band. He holds his clarinet nervously. As the director's white glove raises up. Cliff's heart skips a beat. He has dreamed of this moment and it is finally here. He is a member of the marching band.

   a. Cliff's first football game as a band member
   b. Excitement on the night of the first game
   c. Cliff and his friends at the football game

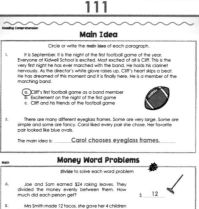

2. There are many different eyeglass frames. Some are very large. Some are simple and some are fancy. Carol liked every pair she chose. Her favorite pair looked like blue ovals.

The main idea is: **Carol chooses eyeglass frames.**

Money Word Problems

Divide to solve each word problem

A. Joe and Sam earned $24 raking leaves. They divided the money evenly between them. How much did each person get?   **$ 12**

B. Mrs Smith made 12 tacos. she gave her 4 children an equal number of tacos. How many tacos did each child receive?   **3 tacos**

C. Jamie and Eddie bought a pack of art paper. The pack contained 20 pieces of paper. If they each take the same amount of paper, how many pieces will they each get?   **10 pieces**

D. Randi has a package of candy containing 49 pieces. If she wanted to eat an equal share of the candy every day for 7 days. how many pieces would she eat each day?   **7 pieces**

114

Identifying Misspelled Words

Underline the spelling error in each sentence. Write the correct spelling on the line.

1. Missy tripped while she was runing. — running
2. Do you beleeve that story? — believe
3. Valentine's Day is in Febuary. — February
4. I take gymnastics classes on Wensdays. — Wednesday
5. Mother made apple pie for desert. — dessert
6. I like to walk to scool. — school
7. Sara is going to the beech on Saturday. — beach
8. It is cool outside, so I will wear a sweter. — sweater

Adding Fractions

Add the fractions.

A. $\frac{6}{8} + \frac{2}{8} = \frac{7}{8}$ B. $\frac{4}{9} + \frac{3}{9} = \frac{7}{9}$ C. $\frac{9}{12} + \frac{1}{12} = \frac{5}{6}$ D. $\frac{1}{6} + \frac{4}{6} = \frac{5}{6}$

E. $\frac{2}{4} + \frac{3}{4} = 1$ F. $\frac{2}{4} + \frac{1}{4} = \frac{3}{4}$ G. $\frac{3}{6} + \frac{1}{6} = \frac{2}{3}$ H. $\frac{1}{6} + \frac{4}{6} = \frac{5}{6}$

119

Words into Math

Use the table to answer the questions.
If the information needed to answer a question is not given, write NG.

Daily Schedule	Time
Homeroom	8:00 – 8:10
1st Period	8:15 – 9:15
2nd Period	9:20 – 10:25
3rd Period	10:25 – 11:25
Lunch	11:25 – 12:00
4th Period	12:00 – 1:15
5th Period	1:05 – 2:05
6th Period	2:10 – 3:10

Charles High School has this daily schedule. It names all the class periods and gives the time each one starts and ends.

1. How long is each class period?   **1 hour**
2. During what period does Ms. Smith teach gym?   **NG**
3. If Jimmy gets to class at 8:30, how much of 1st period has he missed?   **15 minutes**
4. How long is the lunch period?   **35 minutes**
5. What class does Susan have 4th period?   **NG**
6. Which period begins at 9:20?   **2nd Period**
7. Kaitlin's mom picked her up at 2:00. During what period did she leave?   **5th Period**
8. What event happens between 8:00 and 8:10 each morning?   **Homeroom**
9. Jamal stays in Mr. Wood's room for 2nd and 3rd periods. How long is he in that room?   **2 hours**
10. If school is over after 6th period, what time do the students get out?   **3:10**

120

Division Facts 4-12 Review

Divide to solve each problem.

A. $9\overline{)90}$ = 10   B. $10\overline{)20}$ = 2   C. $11\overline{)99}$ = 9   D. $12\overline{)108}$ = 9   E. $11\overline{)77}$ = 7

F. $12\overline{)24}$ = 2   G. $10\overline{)60}$ = 6   H. $12\overline{)60}$ = 5   I. $11\overline{)110}$ = 10   J. $10\overline{)120}$ = 12

K. $9\overline{)27}$ = 3   L. $9\overline{)9}$ = 1   M. $10\overline{)120}$ = 12   N. $11\overline{)121}$ = 11   O. $9\overline{)108}$ = 12

Topic Sentence

A **topic sentence** is a sentence in a paragraph that tells the main idea.

Example: Ellen disliked all types of tiny, crawling things. Spiders made her crazy. Worms gave her the willies. Little, shiny lizards made Ellen feel awful. The only tiny, crawling thing Ellen liked was her little brother Ned.

Read each paragraph. Underline the topic sentence.

1. Raccoons sleep all day. They wake up at night to get food when they are hungry. Fireflies blink on and off at night. Owls hunt for their food after the sun goes down. Bats search for insects after dark. These are all night creatures.

2. There are many interesting things at the hairstyling shop. There is the stylist's chair that spins around and goes up and down. There are all the different combs, lotions, and special things the stylist uses. Some people like the magazines in the waiting area. Some folks like the hair styles they get the best!

3. The takeoff was surprisingly smooth. The sky was clear and there were only a few clouds. The flight attendants were all very friendly. Amanda thought her dinner on the plane was delicious. In fact, everything about Amanda's first airplane ride was perfect.

122

Math Puzzle

Solve the problems below and write the answers in the boxes. On the building, shade in the squares that match your answers. The answers will make a pattern.

$5 \times 3 - 6 =$ **9**
$27 \div 3 + 4 =$ **13**
$3 \times 6 \div 9 =$ **2**
$120 \div 10 \times 11 =$ **132**
$32 \div 8 + 7 =$ **11**
$4 \times 3 - 9 =$ **3**
$2 \times 3 \times 5 =$ **30**
$21 \div 7 + 4 =$ **7**
$81 \div 9 + 8 =$ **17**
$3 \times 2 + 8 =$ **14**
$40 \div 5 + 8 =$ **16**
$56 \div 7 + 7 =$ **15**
$5 \times 8 \div 10 =$ **4**
$4 \times 9 \div 3 =$ **12**
$2 \times 1 \times 3 =$ **6**
$33 \div 11 - 6 =$

8	34	45	27
25	18	19	51
	40	23	
	70	92	
	10	67	
	53	32	
20	22	83	36
20	60	33	78

123

Answer Key

Solve the Code

Math

You must solve the code to find the alligator's name and cross the stream.
For each answer in the code, write the letter of the corresponding problem.

N $\frac{233\ R1}{4\ \overline{)933}}$	E $\frac{116\ R2}{8\ \overline{)930}}$	N $\frac{146\ R2}{5\ \overline{)732}}$	I $\frac{304\ R1}{3\ \overline{)913}}$	D $\frac{110\ R4}{9\ \overline{)994}}$

M $\frac{163\ R2}{6\ \overline{)980}}$	A $\frac{168\ R4}{5\ \overline{)844}}$	S $\frac{413\ R1}{2\ \overline{)827}}$	H $\frac{103\ R2}{9\ \overline{)933}}$	W $\frac{114\ R4}{7\ \overline{)802}}$

S $\frac{133\ R3}{7\ \overline{)934}}$	I $\frac{167\ R2}{3\ \overline{)503}}$	E $\frac{126\ R3}{6\ \overline{)759}}$	R $\frac{122\ R5}{8\ \overline{)981}}$	A $\frac{173\ R2}{4\ \overline{)694}}$

H I S   N A M E
103 R6 304 R1 133 R3   233 R1 173 R2 163 122 R3

I S
167 R2 413 R1

A N D R E W
168 R4 146 R2 110 R4 122 R5 116 R2 114 R4

125

Topic Sentence

A **topic sentence** is a sentence in a paragraph that tells the main idea.
Underline the topic sentence in each paragraph.

1. <u>Learning to play the piano was not always easy for Todd.</u> He did not always like practicing. Sometimes he made a lot of mistakes, even when he was trying hard. Some days, Todd would feel too tired to play. When Todd did start to get better, though, he was very proud.

2. Kim and Kurt spent $10 each for their stamp albums. Kim bought four special stamps from France. They cost $1 each. Kurt spent $6 on a set of Olympic stamps. <u>Collecting stamps was going to be expensive for the children!</u>

3. <u>Winters can be very hard in Vermont.</u> There are often heavy snowfalls with high winds. It can be days before some back roads are plowed. Many people in Vermont chop their own wood. That's very hard work. Many people drive special cars and trucks to get around on the snowy roads.

Math

Adding Fractions

Add. Write each answer in simplest form. The first one has been done for you.

A. $\frac{2}{5} + \frac{1}{5} = \boxed{\frac{3}{5}}$ B. $\frac{3}{5} + \frac{1}{5} = \boxed{\frac{4}{5}}$

C. $\frac{7}{9} + \frac{1}{9} = \boxed{\frac{8}{9}}$ D. $\frac{1}{5} + \frac{2}{5} = \boxed{\frac{3}{5}}$

E. $\frac{3}{8} + \frac{4}{8} = \boxed{\frac{7}{8}}$ F. $\frac{5}{7} + \frac{1}{7} = \boxed{\frac{6}{7}}$

F. $\frac{1}{4} + \frac{3}{4} = \boxed{1}$ G. $\frac{5}{6} + \frac{2}{6} = \boxed{1\frac{1}{6}}$

126

Math

Fraction Addition

Add. Write each answer in simplest form. The first one has been done for you.

A. $\frac{1}{6} + \frac{1}{6} = \boxed{\frac{1}{3}}$ B. $\frac{3}{10} + \frac{1}{10} = \boxed{\frac{2}{5}}$

C. $\frac{1}{7} + \frac{3}{7} = \boxed{\frac{4}{7}}$ D. $\frac{6}{7} + \frac{3}{7} = \boxed{1\frac{2}{7}}$

E. $\frac{1}{8} + \frac{3}{8} = \boxed{\frac{1}{2}}$ F. $\frac{2}{9} + \frac{5}{9} = \boxed{\frac{7}{9}}$

G. $\frac{5}{9} + \frac{1}{9} = \boxed{\frac{2}{3}}$ H. $\frac{2}{5} + \frac{3}{5} = \boxed{1}$

Grammar

Adjectives

Find and underline the **adjectives** in each paragraph.

1. Anna went to the <u>big</u> <u>shoe</u> store with her mother. Anna needed some <u>new</u> shoes. She saw <u>black</u>, <u>shiny</u> shoes and <u>white</u>, <u>ruffled</u> shoes. Anna especially liked the <u>fancy</u> <u>red</u> <u>dress</u> shoes with <u>black</u> and <u>white</u> trim. Anna decided to buy some <u>tan</u> shoes. Anna's mother paid the <u>tall</u> salesman, and Anna wore her <u>new</u> shoes home.

2. I like to watch the <u>brave</u> firefighters work. They wear <u>large</u>, <u>protective</u> outfits to keep them safe from fire. Firefighters try to save <u>small</u> houses, <u>big</u> houses, and <u>office</u> buildings. They will put out a fire anywhere. Sometimes, I have watched them put out fires in the <u>tall</u> forest behind my neighborhood. I would like to be a <u>brave</u> firefighter when I grow up.

127

Writing

Writing in the Third Person

This story is written from the first person **point of view**. Rewrite the story below, changing the point of view to third person. Add an ending to the story.

A Skating Disaster

I was skating on the sidewalk a few blocks from my house yesterday afternoon when a dog darted out of the bushes. The dog ran right across my path. Boom! Down I fell! I stood up and brushed myself off. Suddenly, a little boy ran out of the same bushes. The boy was calling, "Come back, Pixie!" As he rushed past me, I fell down again. I had just picked myself up again when a man raced out of the bushes! He was shouting, "Come back, Sergio! Come back, Pixie!" I . . .

Rosa was skating on the sidewalk a few blocks from her house yesterday afternoon when a dog darted out of the bushes. The dog ran right across her path. Boom! Down she fell! Rosa stood up and brushed herself off. Suddenly, a little boy ran out of the same bushes. The boy was calling, "Come back, Pixie!" As he rushed past Rosa, she fell down again. Rosa had just picked herself up again when a man raced out of the bushes! He was shouting, "Come back, Sergio! Come back, Pixie!" Rosa. . .

Stories will vary.

128

Language Arts

Analogies

Compare the relationships of the words below.
Write a word on the line to complete each analogy.

1. car : driver :: plane : **pilot**
2. bird : sky :: fish : **ocean**
3. coffee : drink :: hamburger : **food**
4. small : tiny :: large : **huge**
5. glove : hand :: boot : **foot**
6. easy : simple :: hard : **difficult**
7. breakfast : lunch :: morning : **noon**
8. blue : color :: round : **shape**
9. date : calendar :: time : **clock**
10. win : lose :: stop : **go**

Math

Subtracting Fractions

Subtract. Write each answer in simplest form. The first one has been done for you.

A. $\frac{2}{3} - \frac{1}{3} = \boxed{\frac{1}{3}}$ B. $\frac{7}{9} - \frac{5}{9} = \boxed{\frac{2}{9}}$

C. $\frac{3}{7} - \frac{1}{7} = \boxed{\frac{2}{7}}$ D. $\frac{3}{5} - \frac{1}{5} = \boxed{\frac{2}{5}}$

E. $\frac{5}{8} - \frac{2}{8} = \boxed{\frac{3}{8}}$ F. $\frac{3}{4} - \frac{1}{4} = \boxed{\frac{1}{2}}$

G. $\frac{8}{9} - \frac{3}{9} = \boxed{\frac{5}{9}}$ H. $\frac{4}{6} - \frac{2}{6} = \boxed{\frac{1}{3}}$

129

Math

Mixed Problem Puzzle

Solve the problems. Use the number key at the bottom of the page to color the picture.

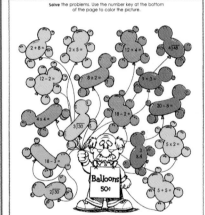

10 = yellow   16 = orange
15 = green   12 = purple

130

Language Arts

Completing Analogies

Fill in the blanks to complete the **analogies**.

1. Ice is to cold as steam is to **heat**
2. The sun is to daytime as the moon is to **nighttime**
3. Perspiration is to heat as shivering is to **cold**
4. Birds are to flying as dolphins are to **swimming**
5. Books are to reading as radios are to **listening**
6. Shoes are to feet as gloves are to **hands**

Math

Subtracting Fractions

Subtract the fractions. Write each answer in simplest form.

A. $\frac{6}{7} - \frac{2}{7} = \frac{4}{7}$ B. $\frac{6}{9} - \frac{3}{9} = \frac{1}{3}$ C. $\frac{9}{10} - \frac{5}{10} = \frac{2}{5}$ D. $\frac{5}{8} - \frac{2}{8} = \frac{3}{4}$

E. $\frac{3}{4} - \frac{1}{4} = \frac{1}{2}$ F. $\frac{2}{5} - \frac{1}{5} = \frac{1}{5}$ G. $\frac{8}{9} - \frac{7}{9} = \frac{7}{9}$ H. $\frac{2}{3} - \frac{1}{3} = \frac{1}{3}$

131

Writing

Writing in the First Person

This story is written from the third person **point of view**. Rewrite the story, changing the point of view to first person. Add an ending to the story.

Soccer Hero

Joey has been playing soccer for three years. His team is called the Mountain Lions. Joey plays goalie on the team. A goalie tries to keep the other team from scoring by standing in front of the net and blocking any balls kicked toward it. Joey is a great goalie. He played on the All-Star Team last year. Last Thursday, the Mountain Lions played a team called the Blazing Suns. The Suns were ahead by two goals. The game was almost over and it looked like the Lions were going to lose. Joey . . .

I have been playing soccer for three years. My team is called the Mountain Lions. I play goalie on the team. A goalie tries to keep the other team from scoring by standing in front of the net and blocking any balls kicked toward it. I am a great goalie. I played on the All-Star Team last year. Last Thursday, the Mountain Lions played a team called the Blazing Suns. The Suns were ahead by two goals. The game was almost over and it looked like the Lions were going to lose. I . . .

Stories will vary.

132

Writing

Proofreading

Circle each letter that should be capitalized.
Add punctuation marks in the proper places.
Write an ending to the story.

Creature from Outer Space

Ⓣim and Ⓘ decided to camp out in the backyard. Ⓦe got our sleeping bags two flashlights and some snacks. Ⓦe unrolled our sleeping bags, lay down, and began to munch on some pretzels. Ⓘt was a clear night and the stars were sparkling brightly. Ⓦe found the Ⓑig Ⓓipper and the Ⓝorth Ⓢtar. Ⓞne bright star seemed to be moving. Ⓦe watched it race across the sky. Ⓢuddenly, it stopped and began to grow bigger. Ⓘt was coming toward us. Ⓘt came to a stop right over our heads. Ⓝow we could see that it was not a star at all. Ⓘt was a spaceship. Ⓐ beam of light shot from the spaceship and glowed all around. Ⓣim . . .

133

157

Answer Key

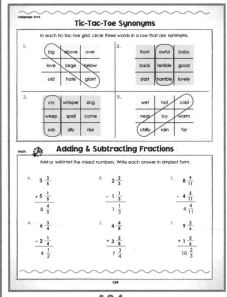

Tic-Tac-Toe Synonyms

In each tic-tac-toe grid, circle three words in a row that are synonyms.

1.
big	above	over
love	large	below
old	hate	giant

2.
front	awful	baby
back	terrible	good
start	horrible	lovely

3.
cry	whisper	sing
weep	spell	come
sob	silly	rise

4.
wet	hot	cold
near	icy	warm
chilly	rain	far

Adding & Subtracting Fractions

Add or subtract the mixed numbers. Write each answer in simplest form.

A. $3\frac{3}{5} + 5\frac{1}{5} = 8\frac{4}{5}$

B. $2\frac{2}{3} - 1\frac{1}{3} = 1\frac{1}{3}$

C. $8\frac{9}{11} - 4\frac{5}{11} = 4\frac{4}{11}$

D. $6\frac{3}{4} - 2\frac{1}{4} = 4\frac{1}{2}$

E. $4\frac{4}{8} + 3\frac{2}{8} = 7\frac{3}{4}$

F. $9\frac{2}{6} + 1\frac{2}{6} = 10\frac{2}{3}$

134

Mixed Problems <, >, or =

Read each problem. Write the correct symbol (<, >, or =) on the line.

A. 60.5 > 60

B. 6 x 4 = 8 x 3

C. 3,345 < 4,002

D. 95 > 93

E. 72.5 > 72.1

F. 40 x 2 > 3 x 30

G. 145,092 < 147,958

H. $\frac{8}{9}$ > $\frac{7}{9}$

I. 50.3 > 50.2

J. 97.05 < 97.50

K. $\frac{12}{12}$ = $\frac{8}{8}$

135

Words into Math

Read the story and answer the questions below.
If the information needed to answer a question is not given, write NG.

Mrs. Grom's fourth grade class is going on a field trip to the zoo. There are 25 students in her class. Each child must pay $2.00 to get into the zoo and $1.27 for bus fare. The class left the school at 9:00 A.M. and returned at 2:20 P.M.

1. What was the total each student paid to go on this trip?
$ 3.27

2. How much money did Mrs. Grom collect from the class altogether?
$ 81.75

3. One parent for every 5 students came along on the trip. How many parents came?
5

4. Did Daniel like the sharks or the polar bears better?
NG

5. How long was the class gone from school?
5 hours, 20 minutes

6. How much did the zoo collect for all 25 students?
$ 50.00

7. How much more did it cost each child to get into the zoo than to ride the bus?
73¢

8. Did the students behave nicely on this trip?
NG

136

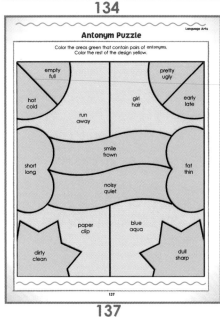

Antonym Puzzle

Color the areas green that contain pairs of antonyms.
Color the rest of the design yellow.

empty full
pretty ugly
hot cold
girl hair
early late
run away
smile frown
short long
fat thin
noisy quiet
paper clip
blue aqua
dirty clean
dull sharp

137

Measure Sense

Using the chart, circle the measurement choice that is most reasonable.

STANDARD LENGTH
Inch (in.): the diameter of a quarter
Foot (ft.): from your shoulder to elbow
Yard (yd.): length of a teacher's desk
Mile (mi.): a short car ride

A. length of a football field — 100 yd.
B. width of a math book — 8 in.
C. height of a fence — 4 ft.
D. height of a desk — 2 in.
E. height of a doorway — 7 ft.
F. width of your wrist — 7 ft.
G. length of a parking lot — 50 yd.
H. length of your foot — 7 in.

Conversion Excursion

Use the conversion chart to complete the statements below.

Standard Length
12 in. = 1 ft.
3 ft. = 1 yd.
5,280 ft. = 1 mi.
1,760 yd. = 1 mi.

24 in. = 2 ft.
6 yd. = 18 ft.
12 ft. = 4 yd.

10,560 ft. = 2 mi.
36 in. = 3 ft.
60 in. = 5 ft.

48 in. = 4 ft.
1 yd. = 36 in.
5 yd. = 15 ft.

36 ft. = 12 yd.
1 ft. = 12 in.
10 ft. = 120 in.

138

Spelling Assessment

Read each group of words. Mark the word that is not spelled correctly.

1. several / skirt / X spiret / strain / torn
2. yawn / yourselves / wow / X wastfe / twin
3. tomato / sword / stole / X sparkel / sixth
4. serve / X ruber / rear / prepare / pinch
5. pad / X neklace / mess / knife / hero
6. footprint / fern / X dozzen / degree / create
7. coast / cellar / broom / X behav / attention

8. gloom / footstep / envelope / drag / X creeture
9. cent / belly / X wastfe / address / account
10. avenue / X bufalo / colorful / croak / dentist
11. X dredful / event / fifty / forward / goodbye
12. guy / history / ink / lace / glitter
13. pale / X sadle / shady / slam / stray
14. tan / taugh / X undergroun / warmth / tin

15. mist / nibble / place / X pitcher / princess
16. rust / skunk / spit / fame / X yesterday
17. warn / twice / tip / X stir / slip
18. rowboat / reddar / pill / package / neat
19. X merry / load / herd / guide / glitter
20. ache / X awakken / birdhouse / buggy / charm
21. comb / crocodile / department / examine / gym

22. actual / acorn / aim / X award / birth
23. chatter / comfort / X crooke / depend / drift
24. example / fought / haircut / X insist / laid
25. lung / mister / noble / X plannet / sadness
26. X shaggy / slant / spit / tangle / tour
27. sort / single / X September / ray / lizard
28. helpless / X geust / glide / football / female

143

Narrative Passage

Read the story, then read each question. Read all the answers and mark the space for the answer you think is right. Mark NH (not here) if the answer can not be figured out from the given information.

Lillian slid lower in her chair. She was almost under her desk. If she could just disappear, maybe the teacher wouldn't call on her. Lillian was prepared. She loved to read and had finished the book two weeks ago. She also liked to write, so the book report was no problem. Lillian did not want to read her report to the class. Her stomach felt sick and her face got hot every time she thought about standing up in front of all those children. The teacher called Lillian's name. Lillian slowly stood up and shuffled to the front of the room. She thought about Sam, a character in her book. If only she could be as brave as he was. Suddenly, Lillian knew what to do! She closed her eyes and pretended she was Sam. She told Sam's story, just as if it had happened to her. When she was finished, Lillian opened her eyes and looked at the class in front of her. They were clapping wildly because she had given such a good report! The teacher was very happy and gave Lillian an A+ on her report. Lillian was happy, too!

1. Why was Lillian trying to hide under her desk?
X She did not want to give the report.
○ She was not feeling well.
○ She always hid under there.
○ NH

2. Lillian was afraid of something. What was she afraid of?
○ reading aloud
X standing up in front of the class
○ her teacher
○ NH

3. Why did the teacher make Lillian give the report?
○ She didn't like Lillian.
○ It was Lillian's turn to report.
○ She wanted Lillian to be brave.
X NH

4. How did Lillian help herself get through the report?
○ She pretended she was at home.
○ She pretended to be brave.
X She pretended to be Sam.
○ NH

5. What words from the story give clues about how Lillian felt giving book reports in front of the class?
○ brave, pretended, wildly
○ happy, character, problem
X disappear, sick, shuffled
○ NH

6. What grade did Lillian get for her report?
X A+
○ E+
○ A
○ NH

144

Vocabulary Assessment

Read the first part of the sentence and look at the underlined word or phrase. Choose the word that means about the same thing as the underlined word or phrase. Mark the correct answer.

1. To make something look larger is to . . .
○ shovel
X lighten
○ magnify

2. To save something is to . . .
X preserve
○ outwit
○ lasso

3. Something that is strong and solid is . . .
○ hoarse
X sturdy
○ harmful

4. Something evil or bad is . . .
X wicked
○ mischief
○ slender

5. To surprise greatly is to . . .
○ astonish
○ cradle
○ involve

6. To sort or put things into categories is to . . .
○ educate
X insult
○ display

7. A strong feeling of wanting to know or learn is . . .
○ lark
X curiosity
○ harmony

8. Something that has no feeling is . . .
○ society
○ mixture
X numb

9. A smell or odor is a . . .
○ humor
○ dipper
X scent

10. A person visiting a new place is a . . .
○ twitch
○ runaway
X tourist

11. To move forward is to . . .
X advance
○ salute
○ skim

12. Something that has a strong, unpleasant taste is . . .
○ fiery
X bitter
○ crimson

13. The power to work or be active is . . .
X energy
○ display

14. A motion made with the arms is a . . .
○ freckle
X gesture
○ custodian

15. Something is to . . .
X budge
○ dimple
○ fend

16. To worry is to be . . .
X concerned
○ lame
○ eerie

17. A strong dislike that makes you feel sick is called . . .
○ length
X disgust
○ reflection

18. Something very good is . . .
○ shatter
X modest
○ fantastic

19. A person who tells the truth is . . .
X honest
○ beaten

20. To want what others have is to be . . .
○ classical
X jealous

21. A smell is an . . .
○ apple
X odor
○ crime

145

Place Value with Large Numbers

Use the given number to find the place values. The first one has been done for you.

1. The number is: **7,320,194,685**
a. Name the digit in the tens place. — 9
b. Name the digit in the tenths place. — 6
c. Name the digit in the millions place. — 0
d. Name the digit in the ones place. — 4
e. In what place value is the digit 0? — thousands
f. In what place value is the digit 2? — ten thousands
g. In what place value is the digit 3? — hundred thousands
h. In what place value is the digit 5? — thousandths

2. The number is: **8,635.147**
a. Name the digit in the hundreds place. — 6
b. Name the digit in the hundredths place. — 4
c. Name the digit in the thousands place. — 8
d. Name the digit in the tenths place. — 1
e. Name the number that is one hundred more. — 8,735.147
f. Name the number that is one thousand less. — 7,635.147
g. Name the number that is one-hundredth less. — 8,635.137
h. Name the number that is one more. — 8,636.147

3. The number is: **1,320,796.485**
a. Name the digit in the millions place. — 1
b. Name the digit in the ones place. — 6
c. Name the digit in the thousandths place. — 5
d. Name the digit in the ten thousands place. — 2
e. Name the number that is one-thousand less. — 1,310,796.485
f. Name the number that is one-thousandth more. — 1,320,796.486
g. Name the number that is one million less. — 1,320,795.485
h. Name the number that is one million more. — 2,320,796.485

146

158

Cut-and-Color Awards

Parent: Have your child decorate and color these awards. Fill in your child's name and the date to mark each accomplishment. The awards can be worn as badges or put into small frames.

I understand analogies!

Name: _____ Date: _____

I can multiply LARGE numbers!

Name: _____ Date: _____

I can identify the topic sentence in a paragraph!

Name: _____ Date: _____

I know my math facts!

Name: _____ Date: _____

I can divide LARGE numbers!

Name: _____ Date: _____

nouns verbs adverbs

I know my parts of speech!

adjectives

Name: _____ Date: _____

I can use punctuation correctly!

Name: _____ Date: _____

I understand synonyms, homonyms, and antonyms!

Name: _____ Date: _____